As ___

Thomas Cook ___ experts in travel.

For more than 135 years our
guidebooks have unlocked the secrets
of destinations around the world,
sharing with travellers a wealth of
experience and a passion for travel.

**Rely on Thomas Cook as your
travelling companion on your next trip
and benefit from our unique heritage.**

Thomas Cook **traveller** guides

ICELAND
Lindsay Bennett

Thomas
Cook

Your travelling companion since 1873

Written by Lindsay Bennett, updated by Laura Dixon
Original photography by Pete Bennett

914.91
Ic15t
2011
3rd ed.

Published by Thomas Cook Publishing
A division of Thomas Cook Tour Operations Limited
Company registration no. 3772199 England
The Thomas Cook Business Park, 9 Coningsby Road,
Peterborough PE3 8SB, United Kingdom
Email: sales@thomascook.com, Tel: + 44 (0)1733 416477
www.thomascookpublishing.com

Produced by Cambridge Publishing Management Limited
Burr Elm Court, Main Street, Caldecote CB23 7NU
www.cambridgepm.co.uk

ISBN: 978-1-84848-343-9

Series Editor: Karen Beaulah
Production/DTP: Steven Collins

Printed and bound in Spain by GraphyCems

Cover photography © Giovanni Simeone/SIME-4Corners Images Ltd

Although every care has been taken in compiling this publication, and the
contents are believed to be correct at the time of printing, Thomas Cook Tour
Operations Limited cannot accept any responsibility for errors or omissions,
however caused, or for changes in details given in the guidebook, or for the
consequences of any reliance on the information provided. Descriptions and
assessments are based on the author's views and experiences when writing and
do not necessarily represent those of Thomas Cook Tour Operations Limited.

Contents

Introduction

Iceland is a land of extremes: glaciers and molten lava; midnight sun and days full of night; a fascinating history and a forward-thinking population. Whether you explore its history, culture, natural attractions or adrenalin sports, you won't find anything like it anywhere else in the world; Iceland is a real one-off.

This is nature writ large – stark and strong, always alluring and never boring. Vast cliffs, glorious beaches, the world's largest lava fields, glaciers and waterfalls at every turn, thousands of hectares of moors and tundra, and seemingly endless tracts of high desert plains only scratch the surface of what is on offer.

This panoply is further enhanced by the play of light and shadow across the landscape, giving the effect of constant movement and inducing an array of colours in mosses, heathers and rocks.

Turf houses in the Western Fjords

More fascinating than the surface beauty are the primeval elements at work just below. No matter what their age, humans cannot fail to be impressed by its super-hot fumaroles, powerful geysers and bubbling mud pools – this is our planet earth at its rawest and when faced with such monstrous power just below our feet we feel humbled and small.

Movement on land is mirrored by movement offshore; Iceland cannot be discussed without reference to the sea. There are myriad languid coastal inlets, while the flotsam and jetsam of the Atlantic fetches up on beaches during winter gales and its waves pound incessantly all the year round at the base of cliffs in the Westfjords. The sea brought Icelanders to this land and its bounty sustains them to this day and encourages fierce political debate.

Vatnajökull glacier

Iceland's human history is no less epic. A freedom-loving seafaring race driven from their lands by a ruthless monarchy, they made a living here through sheer grit and hard work, and then went on to develop one of the world's earliest parliamentary democracies. This is a people whose oral tradition was recorded as soon as quill and vellum arrived on the island, so we can follow every twist and turn in the fascinating narrative.

Today, after centuries as farmers and fishermen, Icelanders have embraced the modern age with gusto. With the help of technology – and particularly with the advent of the Internet – they are no longer a remote outcrop on Europe's northwestern boundary. The capital, Reykjavík, is dynamic and forward-thinking. Though small by international standards, it punches above its weight in cultural terms.

In recent years, economic collapse and an active volcano have stopped Europe in its tracks, but beyond the headlines, this small country, the size of Wales, has much more to offer. The landscape, unpolluted environment and stunning views will delight even the most jaded of travellers. With other-worldly experiences around every corner, you'll be sure to have a trip to remember.

The land

Iceland has one of the most fascinating geologies in the world. Even a layperson cannot help but be drawn to the elemental forces of creation at work here. Iceland is a newborn land straddling the European and continental plates, and nowhere else is the earth's crust as thin as it is here.

The great misnomer

Norse settler Flóki Vilgarðarson is responsible for Iceland's name. After a rather easy summer in the country, a harsh winter took him by surprise and killed all his livestock. He cursed the Land of Ice, or *Ísland*, and the name stuck. Never mind that nearby Greenland is icy and Iceland, as visitors quickly realise, is mainly green. Only 11 per cent of the land is covered year-round in ice, including Vatnajökull glacier, the largest glacier mass in Europe.

The epithet 'Land of Fire and Ice' is more appropriate, given that 100 per cent of the land is volcanic in origin and 30 per cent is still active. There are regular earthquakes and eruptions, the most recent being in 2010 when ash from the volcano under Eyjafjallajökull glacier caused chaos throughout European airspace.

The youngest parts of Iceland are the highly volcanic areas in the centre, southeast and the ridge along the Reykjanes Peninsula. Surtsey, an island in the Westman Islands chain off the south coast of Iceland, is the very newest. Created by an undersea volcano in 1963, it is a UNESCO World Heritage Site.

An iceberg near Fjallsjökull

Iceland

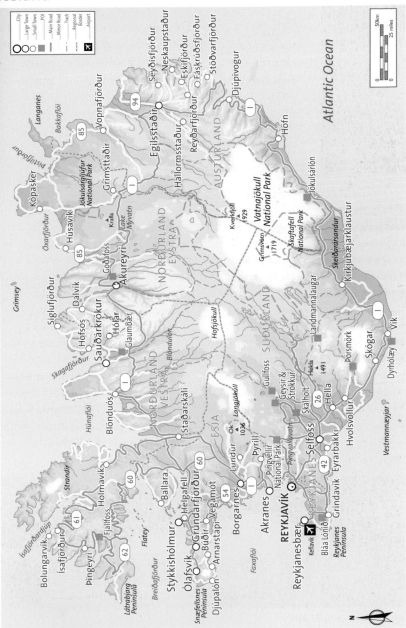

Legend:
- City
- Large Town
- Small Town
- POI
- Main Road
- Minor Road
- Track
- Regional
- Border
- Airport

50km
25 miles

Atlantic Ocean

Langanes
Bakkaflói
Þistilfjörður
Seyðisfjörður
Neskaupstaður
Eskifjörður
Fáskrúðsfjörður
Stöðvarfjörður
Djúpivogur
Vopnafjörður
Öxarfjörður
Kópasker
Egilsstaðir
Hallormsstaður
Reyðarfjörður
AUSTURLAND
Höfn
Grímsstaðir
Jökulsárlón
Jökulsárgljúfur National Park
Húsavík
Lake Mývatn
Krafla
Kverkfjöll 1929
Vatnajökull National Park
Skaftafell National Park
Grímsey
Siglufjörður
Dalvík
Godafoss
Akureyri
NORÐURLAND EYSTRA
Grímsvötn 1719
Skeiðarársandur
Kirkjubæjarklaustur
Hofsós
Hólar
Glaumbær
Sauðárkrókur
Blönduós
Hofsjökull
SUÐURLAND
Landmannalaugar
Skagafjörður
NORÐURLAND VESTRA
Blöndulón
Þórsmörk
Skógar
Vík
Hekla 1491
Húnaflói
Staðarskáli
Langjökull
Gullfoss
Geysir & Strokkur
Skálholt
Hella
Dyrhólaey
Strandir
Hólmavík
ESJA
1036
Pyrill
Hvolsvöllur
Ísafjarðardjúp
Bolungarvík
Ísafjörður
Þingeyri
Fjallfoss
Flatey
Ballara
Helgafell
Grundarfjörður
Vegamót
Lundur
Þingvellir
National Park
Þingvallavatn
Selfoss
Eyrarbakki
Vestmannaeyjar
Breiðafjörður
Stykkishólmur
Ólafsvík
Búðir
Arnarstapi
Djúpalón
Borgarnes
Akranes
REYKJANES
Grindavík
Látrabjarg Peninsula
Snæfellsnes Peninsula
REYKJAVÍK
Reykjanesbær
Keflavík
Blá Lónið
Reykjanes Peninsula
Faxaflói

85
94
85
61
60
60
54
62
42
26

N

The land

Landscape

Iceland's landscape is ever-changing and always impressive. Vast, dark and menacing magma flows, sheer cliffs, stark upland moors, pendulous scree slopes, active volcanoes, seemingly somnolent glaciers, unpredictable geysers, steaming and smelly fumaroles, and starkly beautiful black sand beaches – a true feast for the eyes!

Besides fire and ice, another factor that is elemental in Iceland's landscape is water. It is always on the move, sustaining spawning salmon in rivers or dropping in dramatic roaring waterfalls to the sea beyond.

Much of Iceland's landscape is magnificent and challenging rather than pretty, and much of it has never been conquered by humans. But where they have managed to gain a foothold, neat farmsteads have sprung up, often

A view of Lake Þingvallavatn

in the lea of hills or in coastal knolls. Tiny Lutheran churches further stake man's claim.

Flora and fauna

There's a joke in Iceland: 'What do you do if you find yourself lost in an Icelandic forest? Stand up!' The island is almost devoid of trees and most of the vegetation rises only a metre or so above the ground. But this wasn't always so. When settlers first arrived, up to 40 per cent of Iceland had a cover of trees and the timber was soon put to work as raw material for building houses and boats. What the Norsemen did not realise was that these trees were much slower-growing than in their native Scandinavia, and that their stocks could not be replenished. Grazing sheep further prevented regrowth and in a short time the forests were exhausted. Replanting programmes began in the 20th century but over the last 30 years there has been an increase in concern about the depletion of Icelandic flora with pressure from grazing sheep, horses and reindeer, as well as soil erosion. The island's plant life is more varied close to ground level. There is a profusion of wild herbs including parsley, gentian, mint and mustard, and several berry species, while the lava flows are blanketed by a rich carpet of mosses, lichens, and violet shades of lupina, the wild flower of Iceland.

Iceland is not rich in animals. When the colonists arrived there were only

THOMAS COOK TRAVELLERS ICELAND

This book is divided into a number of geographical areas. The capital, Reykjavík, is where you are likely to start your visit, and is a good place to get acquainted with Iceland's history, cuisine and nightlife.

Next comes a section on places around the capital, covering many of Iceland's most famous and most visited attractions. You can visit these by renting a car or by booking one of the many well-organised trips that depart the year round. If you don't intend to tour the whole country, this section offers you a sampling of historical and natural attractions, to give you a flavour of Iceland.

After this we begin the journey clockwise taking in the attractions of the northwest, north, east and south. Iceland's ring road, route 1, allows easy access between each region. Lastly the 'Getting away from it all' section introduces you to areas off the beaten track.

two mammal species – the co-dependent mouse and the Arctic fox. The waters are rich, with populations of fish, whales and seals, but, without doubt, birds are Iceland's most abundant non-domesticated fauna, both seabirds and migratory birds from Europe and North America. Large herds of introduced reindeer inhabit the uplands of the northeast of the island, and Icelandic horses and sheep (brought over by the settlers) are seen everywhere.

The Icelandic people

Much is made of the Viking legacy in Icelandic blood but it would be true to say that the population is less homogeneous than that. Simply look at a cross-section of the people and you will see that their hair colour runs from the Scandinavian almost-white/blond through strawberry-blond to brown. The same is true for the eye colour; a good percentage of the population does not have blue eyes.

That is because, in addition to a Norse population, a number of Celts from Scotland, Ireland and the Orkneys were also part of the exodus fleeing the yoke of the Scandinavian monarchy along with their Viking masters – and their genes merged with those from Norway and Sweden.

In 2010, Iceland's population reached 317,630, and nearly all of them are descended from the very first 9th- and 10th-century settlers, making them one of the purest bloodlines in the world.

This information is not just of scientific interest but explains a lot about Icelandic society. Close familial and kinship ties forged over almost a thousand years of community living have recently been fractured by the modernisation of the Icelandic economy, mass migration from other parts of the country to Reykjavík and an exodus to Europe. In 1880, there were only three towns on the island inhabited by just 5 per cent of the total population; the rest lived scattered around the coast. Today, two-thirds of all Icelanders live in or close to the capital and many farms have been abandoned or converted into golf courses.

The land

The ice man cometh:
the power of glaciation

A glacier is a huge river of frozen water formed on land, built up over millennia of ice accumulation and lasting many thousands of years. It is one of the most powerful natural forces on the planet and plays an important role in shaping the Icelandic landscape.

In the past few years, attention has finally been paid to the global warming crisis, and scientists have discovered many Arctic glaciers beginning to break down and melt.

Today, around a tenth of the earth's surface is covered by glacial ice but during the Ice Ages up to 30 per cent was subsumed. During the last Ice Age, the Pleistocene period, Iceland was almost totally buried under thick ice. Today, 11 per cent of the country's land area is covered by glacial ice and its landscape owes much to the power of these cold leviathans.

Fjallsjökull glacier

Glacial erosion

Erosion occurs in two major forms. At the base and sides of the glacier, large amounts of rocky debris and smaller sediment are pulled from the surface of the land, held in place and carried by the constant thawing and refreezing of a thin layer where the ice is in contact with the land. This is called *plucking*.

In a second process, known as *scouring*, the aforementioned rocks and debris held in the ice are dragged over the land as the glacier moves down a hillside, scraping the surface of the rocks and causing marks called *striations*. When working at its most powerful, the immense weight, movement and scouring of the glacier can reduce rocks to an extremely fine flour-like sediment which when mixed with water is known as *glacial milk*.

As erosion continues, a valley becomes deeper and wider over time, and takes on a characteristic U-shape.

Glacial deposition

As a glacier retreats the rocks and other debris or sediment it carried down the valley are deposited on the land. The sediment can simply be dropped directly from the ice (*till*) or

Jökulsárlón glacial lagoon

carried away from the ice by meltwater (*geofluvial deposits*).

When the till forms mounds or ridges it is known as *moraine*. A terminal moraine marks the farthest reach of the glacier. At the side of glaciers lateral moraines are deposited.

Jökulhlaups and sandurs

In Iceland, most glaciers sit atop active volcanoes producing unique glacial phenomena. The most dramatic of these is a *jökulhlaup*, a sudden and dramatic release of glacial meltwater.

Jökulhlaups can be caused by gradual melting of the ice by subcrust heat. This process eventually produces enough meltwater to raise the glacial ice cap and the water drains away through the gap. However, a subglacial volcanic eruption, like that experienced in 2010 under

Eyjafjallajökull glacier, can melt a large amount of glacial ice very quickly, causing an almost immediate flood. In that instance, the nearby population was evacuated due to flood risk.

Whichever way it happens, a *jökulhlaup* transports tonnes of soft sediment out from the glacier base, depositing it on an outwash plain as the surge loses its power. These plains, called *sandurs*, are specific to sites with subglacial volcanoes and the Skeiðarársandur in Iceland (from where the name *sandur* was taken) is the largest in the world. There are many examples of this in Iceland – plains with little vegetation or habitation in the ice of towering volcanic mountains, usually with the affix *-sandur* as part of the area's name. Up to 10m (32ft) of sediment can be deposited on the *sandur* during one *jökulhlaup* event.

History

330 BC   Greek explorer Pytheas sails from Marseilles to find the ends of the earth. He sails north past Great Britain and after six days comes across an island he calls Ultima Thule. It is believed that this was Iceland, but no records remain to confirm the theory.

c. AD 795   Irish monk Dicuil documents the travels of Irish priests to Thule – independent corroboration of the Pytheas text. Dicuil settles in Iceland but no long-term habitation is formed.

c. late 9th century   Harald the Fairhead, king of Norway, routs his enemies on the Scandinavian Peninsula and harries them to the point where they set out to settle beyond his influence. Iceland, known to them as Snæland, is a natural choice.

860   Flóki Vilgarðarson travels to the island, navigating with ravens (*see p6*). He is unimpressed with the place and nicknames it *Ísland* – literally translated as 'Iceland'.

874   Norwegian Ingólfur Arnarson becomes the first recorded settler. A Viking fleeing the Norwegian choke, he farms land in an area he calls Reykjavík, or 'smoky bay', after the steam he saw rising from the hot springs.

930   The Icelandic Alþing, or parliament, is founded to govern the island by consensus. The Icelandic 'Age of Peace', also known as the Saga Age, begins.

985   Eiríkur the Red, father of Leifur Eiríksson, settles in Iceland.

c. 11th century   Leifur Eiríksson discovers a new land to the west. He calls it Vinland. It was either the east coast of northern USA or southern Canada.

1000   Christianity is introduced to Iceland.

1056   Consecration of the first Catholic bishop of Iceland at Skálholt.

1118   The laws of the Alþing are written down for the first time. Also called the end of the 'Age of Peace'.

1120–1220	The 'Age of Writing' – the *Book of the Icelanders* is written at this time.
1230	The civil wars begin. Also known as the 'Age of the Sturlung' after the *Saga* that commits the details to parchment. The political consensus begins to fall apart and private armies roam the land.
1252	King Hákon Hákonarson offers to help control the situation.
1281	Iceland comes under Norwegian rule.
1397	The Kalmar Union between Norway, Denmark and Sweden (three independent nations under one Danish monarch) brings Iceland under Danish influence. The Union is troubled from the start.
1402–4	Black Death ravages the island. Up to two-thirds of the population perish.
1530s	The Kalmar Union breaks apart as Sweden and Denmark play power games. When Denmark imposes rule over Norway it takes control of Iceland.
1540–50	Denmark imposes the Reformation on Iceland causing bloodshed and chaos across the country.
1602	Denmark enforces a trade monopoly on Iceland – goods can go in and out only through Danish companies and trading fleets.
1783–5	Catastrophic volcanic eruptions wreak havoc across Iceland.
1787	Free trade is established in Iceland for Danish subjects but not for Icelanders.
1800	Abolition of the Alþing.
1800s	First stirrings of an Icelandic independence movement. Iceland-born figures such as scholar Jón Sigurðsson lobby for more commercial and political freedom.
1843	Alþing re-established.
1855	Free trade introduced for Icelanders.
1874	King Christian IX of Denmark visits Iceland for the first time to mark the millennium of the foundation of the island. He declares a new Icelandic constitution.

1904	Icelandic home rule is declared under the control of Denmark.
1917	Women are enfranchised.
1918	The Act of Union recognises Icelandic self-determination as a state within the Kingdom of Denmark. The Act is to be reviewed again in 1940.
1940	Germany annexes Denmark. The Icelandic Alþing takes control of Icelandic affairs and declares the island neutral. The British occupy Iceland because of its strategic importance. They build the airfield at Reykjavík.
1941	British forces leave Iceland and American forces arrive.
1944	The independent Republic of Iceland founded on 17 June.
1946	At the end of the war, the Americans ask for approval for several military bases, but their request is rejected by the Icelandic Alþing.
1949	Iceland becomes a founder member of the United Nations but the decision to keep an American-dominated NATO military base on the island is not popular with the population.

1952	Iceland's national waters are extended to 6.4km (4 miles).
1958	Iceland's national waters are extended to 19.3km (12 miles) prompting the first 'Cod War' with Britain.
1963	An underwater volcanic eruption creates the island of Surtsey.
1965	Denmark agrees to return originals of the *Icelandic Sagas* that had been taken to Copenhagen.
1972	Iceland's national waters are extended to 80.5km (50 miles), resulting in the second Cod War.
1973	The eruption of the island of Heimæy prompts an evacuation of the population. Nixon and Pompidou hold a summit in Reykjavík.
1974	1,100 years of inhabitation celebrations. The A1 ring road is completed.
1975	Iceland unilaterally increases its territorial waters to 322km (200 miles), bringing it again into conflict with the British in a third Cod War.

1980	First woman president, Vigdís Finnbogadóttir, is elected.
1982	The International Whaling Commission (a group of whale-hunting nations) calls a moratorium on all hunting to study depleting whale numbers.
1986	Reagan–Gorbachev summit in Reykjavík marks the beginning of the end of the Communist era.
1995	A winter of avalanches kills 34 people in the Westfjords.
2001	Iceland is accepted into the Schengen agreement.
2003	The Icelandic parliament approves the resumption of whaling for research purposes.
2005	Iceland offers controversial American chess player Bobby Fischer political asylum despite the opposition of the US government.
2006	The United States Naval Air Station Keflavík shuts down its operations. Iceland resumes commercial whaling. Its annual quota is 30 minke whales and 9 fin whales.
2007	A law banning smoking in public places comes into effect throughout Iceland. The controversial Kárahnjúkar Dam begins preliminary operations.
2008	Iceland's three largest banks, Glitnir, Landsbanki and Kaupþing, crash with a combined debt of approximately six times the nation's GDP. British savers who invested in high-interest savings accounts in Iceland have their deposits guaranteed by the Bank of England. Long-running disputes continue about when Iceland can reimburse the UK.
2009	Due to the public's dissent over the financial crisis, the government collapses. A new left-wing government is formed a week later.
2010	A small volcano under Eyjafjallajökull glacier erupts. The ash released into the air presents a flight risk across Europe and planes are grounded.
2011	The Icelandic National Concert & Conference Centre and Hotel is set to open at the end of the year.

The Vikings

'… on the 7th of the Ides of January, the havoc of heathen men miserably destroyed God's church at Lindisfarne, through rapine and slaughter.'
THE ANGLO-SAXON CHRONICLE, c. *AD 890*

Until very recently, this was the popular view of the Vikings: savage, pagan brutes who would appear on the horizon in their boats, land and make a lightning raid, rape and pillage, and then depart as quickly as they came, carrying slaves in tow. *The Anglo-Saxon Chronicle* is one of several accounts of Viking activities during the late first millennium and it has coloured our view of these mysterious men of the north. Over the last 20 years, however, new archaeological research has changed our impression of the Vikings. They are now viewed as traders rather than raiders, and sophisticates rather than savages.

This sculpture of Leifur Eiríksson, the Viking chief who discovered America, stands outside Hallgrímskirkja in Reykjavík

Who were the Vikings?

The term 'Viking' is used by scholars to describe the peoples who travelled out of their homeland in Scandinavia to dominate Europe from c. 800–1100. There was never a single united Viking culture – they would have described themselves as Danes, Swedes or Norwegians – but one thing they did have in common was their language – Old Norse.

The Vikings headed west to northern Britain, to Iceland, Greenland, Baffin Island and, it is thought, North America. They ventured south into what is now Normandy in France, and they also travelled east through the Caspian and Black Seas, reaching Constantinople and beyond. They may have raided, but then they also traded and settled; especially in the lands of northwestern Europe.

The Viking ship

The secret of the success of the Viking diaspora was their shipbuilding ability. The crafts they built were the jets of their day. The *drekar*, popularly known as the 'Viking longship', was a dual power vessel with sails and oars.

Viking axeman in wax at the Saga Museum

It was 'clinker built' (with wooden planks overlapping downward, held in place by clinched nails), making it lightweight and flexible, and with a rudder rather than a keel giving the boat a very shallow draught for entering shallow waters.

A *drekar* found at Roskilde Fjord in Denmark was 47m (154ft) long with 72 oars, a 200sq m (2,153sq ft) sail and a draught of only 1m (3ft). It could carry a crew of one hundred.

Viking lifestyles

The Vikings were consummate farmers and traders. They lived in village settlements or farmsteads. The long winters were spent on making handicrafts, which were traded in towns in the summer. While the men were away on trade missions the women would assume full responsibility for all aspects of daily life; but, in general, the responsibilities of men were hunting and fishing while women ran the house, and undertook weaving, spinning and sail-making.

The Viking runes

The Viking runes were an important part of Viking society. They were a set of mystical symbols used to cast spells and reveal the future. The Vikings believed that the runes were revealed to their god Odin (*see pp70–71*) and thus they were imbued with sacred power that could be harnessed for good and evil. Rune masters who could cast and interpret the sacred messages were highly respected by the community.

Later, the runes were used as an alphabet of phonetic sounds that could be put together to form coherent sentences.

Politics

The fierce self-determination and independence of Icelanders come through most clearly in their attitude to politics. You will find very few statues raised to commemorate the leaders and a jovial cynicism about domestic and international statesmen particularly today, post-crash. Yet, there is a passion for social issues and about where Iceland is heading in the future that shows a keen involvement in the political process.

The Alþing

Most early settlers fled to Iceland to escape the regime of the Norwegian monarchy, and in particular the tyranny of Harald the Fairhead whose heavy hand stretched across Scandinavia and into Scotland and Ireland. The early Icelandic population was therefore vehemently egalitarian, anti-monarchy and eschewed rule by any kind of force. However, as the population grew, it became clear that some kind of governing body would be needed to adjudicate in disputes over land and social justice. They solved this problem with a revolutionary new system of government – the Alþing, the world's first parliament.

Founded in AD 930, the Alþing was basically an annual meeting where problems were discussed and resolved, and rules decided by mutual consent. Law-making and debate took place at the *Lögberg* or 'Law Rock', an outcrop in Þingvellir National Park. Here the presiding official elected for the session,

the *Lögsöumaður*, or 'Law Maker', would chair meetings and publicly proclaim any decisions made or laws passed. The meetings were open to all free men but decisions were made by the *Lögrétta* (legislature), which comprised a number of *goðar*, or local leaders, plus the *Lögsöumaður*.

Later, as the system developed, a judiciary was established with the *fimmtardómur* (supreme court) of 48 judges appointed by the *Lögrétta*. In its heyday the annual Alþing was a major social event and a huge fair would accompany the serious business.

With the arrival of Danish rule, the Alþing became a shadow of its former self, acting simply as an enforcement agency of laws enacted by the monarchy in Copenhagen.

The Independence Movement

Jón Sigurðsson (1811–79) is regarded as the father of Icelandic nationalism. The Republic of Iceland was founded on his birthday (17 June) and it is celebrated as National Day. Born in the remote Westfjords, he moved to Copenhagen in 1833 to continue his studies and then went to work in the repository where the originals of the great *Icelandic Sagas* were stored.

Being so close to the 'soul of Iceland' captured his imagination and he began his campaign for Icelandic self-determination. He became the voice of Iceland in Denmark and through carefully phrased verbal argument and a diplomatic approach gradually made his mark with the Danish authorities.

In 1845, by decree of the Danish government, the Icelandic Alþing was reinstated as a legislative body. Suffrage was limited to males over 25 and of independent means – so it was not exactly democratic; its head was Jón Sigurðsson. Though it did initiate legislation on a number of domestic matters, it was still, in essence, an advisory body to the government in Copenhagen.

In 1874, a new Danish constitution granted the Alþing sovereignty over Iceland's internal issues, though the Crown still had the right to veto legislation and often did where it thought the change would conflict with Danish national interest.

Höfði formerly housed the British Embassy and has hosted important political talks

The president's summer residence, Bessastaðir

This was Jón's final triumph as he died five years later.

The momentum carried the process on after his death. In 1904, Iceland was granted home rule and a parliament of 40 members was elected by proportional representation. An Icelandic minister was responsible to the parliament and acted as liaison with Copenhagen. Just after World War I, on 1 December 1918, Iceland became a sovereign state in union with its former colonial master and the Alþing became a national legislative chamber. In 1944, Iceland declared itself an independent parliamentary democracy with a single legislative chamber, the Alþing.

Iceland today

The Alþing currently has sixty-three members with nine members elected from each of the island's six constituencies and the remaining members chosen according to proportional representation to reflect their party's popularity.

General elections take place once every four years, with every citizen over 18 and living in Iceland being eligible to vote. Electoral participation is high.

Iceland's president is elected by popular vote every four years. The current incumbent, Ólafur Ragnar Grímsson, has been in office since 1996.

Parliamentary sessions open on 1 October every year. The first order of business is to elect a president of the Alþing for that session. He or she ensures that the debates and procedure proceed within the rules, and that all opinions are heard. The Alþing sessions are open to the public.

Party politics

Currently, the Alþing power game revolves around these seated parties (listed here in alphabetical order):

The Citizens' Movement (Borgarahreyfingin) – a collective supporting radical change at governmental level in response to the recession. Formed in 2009 with four seats in the Alþing.

The Independence Party (Sjálfstæðisflokkurinn) – a right-wing party supporting NATO membership and opposed to joining the EU.

The Left-Green Party (Vinstrihreyfingin-Grænt Framboð) – a party covering the far left, pro-environment, pro-feminist and anti-NATO concerns.

The Liberal Party (Frjálslyndi Flokkurinn) – a centre-right party with a desire to protect Iceland's traditional rights, especially fishing. Vehemently anti-immigration.

The Movement (Hreyfing) – this party has grown out of the Citizens' Movement.

The Progressive Party (Framsóknarflokkurinn) – a party with a centre-right stance and strong fishing and farming support. The country's second-largest party.

The Social Democrat Alliance Party (Samfylkingin) – a centre-left social democrat mainstream party and since 2009, Iceland's largest party.

Post-crash Iceland

Iceland's parliament was in crisis after its banks collapsed in 2008. Public pressure built on the government with weekly protests; Prime Minister Geir Haarde withdrew from politics for health reasons and the government collapsed in January 2009. A parliamentary election was called in April when the newly created Citizens' Movement won four seats and the Independence Party, which had been in power for 18 years, lost a third of its support. The result was a coalition between the Left-Green, Progressive and Liberal Parties, with Jóhanna Sigurðardóttir as the new prime minister.

The future

To secure its future post-crash, Iceland was forced to ask the IMF for aid; this spectre still hangs over the country, which at the present time owes the Bank of England money after it bailed out investors in the crashed online bank Icesave. Finance will dictate its politics for years to come, and it looks likely that by 2012, the country will be forced to join the euro for financial stability. This will come at quite a cost to the independent nation, not least to its fishing industry.

Culture

'Art isn't put on a pedestal [in Iceland]. It's part of life – like baking a cake.'

Björk
Seventeen *Magazine, August 1997*

Pop diva Björk's quote above sums up the Icelander's approach to the arts. There are very few countries in the world where artistic endeavour is so closely entwined with everyday life, or where art in all its forms is so accessible and understood by ordinary people. Icelanders are comfortable with creativity and this is tied directly to a rich vein of oral and written culture passed down through generations.

As you travel around, you will find that almost every town in Iceland remembers a local hero with a plaque, a statue or a small museum. Invariably, those revered are writers or artists, in stark contrast to the generals and politicians who tend to be honoured in the rest of Europe.

That said, it took many generations for culture and the arts to become a 'profession'. 'Jobbing' artists who wrote

A sculpture at Borgarnes

or painted in between making a living as postmaster, sheriff or farmer were the norm until the late 18th century. Even today many young musicians play for pleasure rather than in the hope of fame, and may delve into several forms of the art rather than specialising in one, as is the norm in most societies.

The legacy of the *Sagas*

The influence that the medieval *Sagas* (*see pp28–9*) still has on the cultural life of modern Iceland cannot be overstated. The *Sagas* were written centuries ago but the Icelandic language has changed little since that time and the stories are still read in their original form by today's population – something that the English cannot do with some of their historic literary masterpieces: *Beowulf* or Chaucer's *Canterbury Tales*, for example. The *Sagas*' recurring themes of the details of everyday life combined with epic trials of human fortitude are picked up by modern writers, painters and film-makers. The mythology of the stories has been infused into the bedrock of the Icelandic belief system, and it finds an outlet in the creativity of passing generations.

Words

Iceland's modern literary giant is Halldór Kiljan Laxness, who was awarded the Nobel Prize for Literature in 1955, the first person to achieve international fame while writing in his native Icelandic. Born Halldór

The original manuscript of the *Sagas*

Helgason, he spent his childhood in the countryside before leaving Iceland to explore the outside world. He converted to Catholicism during a sojourn in France, adopting the name Laxness and the middle name Kiljan after the Irish saint – this became his nom de plume. During this era he also wrote his first major novel, *The Great Weaver of Kashmir*. Soon afterwards he discovered socialism and left religion behind.

A prolific writer with over 60 major works, Laxness wrote his seminal series of books during the 1930s after returning to Iceland, the most prominent being *Independent People*. His novels have a central theme: seen through the eyes of the disenfranchised hero or heroine, the beautifully woven narrative features the recurring problems of poverty, exploitation and an unsympathetic establishment. It is now possible to visit the Laxness house, which has been turned into a small museum (*see p65*).

Carrying on in this literary vein are novelists such as Vigdis Grímsdóttir, Ólafur Jóhann Ólafsson, Guðbergur Bergsson and Hallgrimur Helgason (b. 1959). Helgason's book, *101 Reykjavík*, was turned into a successful film. In many ways, he encapsulates the Icelander's approach to the arts. He is a recognised artist, a stand-up comedian, a cartoonist and a playwright, and sees nothing unusual in this multi-genre approach.

Painting and sculpture

Visit any of the turf and wood farmsteads around the island and it soon becomes clear how adept the Icelanders were and are at carving decoration into wood, bone and horn. This was almost exclusively a cottage industry and there were no full-time artists and no opportunities to study art without moving abroad. Ásgrímur Jónsson (1876–1958) broke the mould when he became Iceland's first professional artist and as the 20th century saw the flowering of modernism, Icelanders embraced the new movements with relish. Jóhannes Sveinsson Kjarval (1885–1972) was Ásgrímur's main peer. His romantic and bohemian lifestyle saw him remain poor throughout the whole of his career despite being fêted during his lifetime. His eccentric approach to life meant he sometimes had to give away

or barter his paintings in return for food and shelter.

The same period also saw the birth of sculpture in Iceland and its two earliest exponents are still highly revered. Einar Jónsson (1874–1954) trained in Copenhagen and Rome but returned to his homeland for long periods. He worked mostly in plaster but since his death, several of his major works have been recast in bronze. Ásmundur Sveinsson (1893–1982) was a couple of decades younger than Einar. He studied in Sweden and was heavily influenced by the arrival of Bauhaus. Later, Sigurjón Ólafsson (1908–82) completes a trio of talent. An experimental artist originally trained as a house painter, he has 18 monumental pieces on display in the capital.

Each of these three artists has museums or galleries dedicated to them in Reykjavík where major works, along with personal effects and workspaces, allow us to enjoy their respective creative talents and approaches.

Today, the visual-arts world in Iceland is vibrant with new genres of photography and electronic media broadening the palate. Erró, born Goðmundur Goðmundersson in 1932, is a leading modern pop-art virtuoso who has donated a number of works to the Reykjavík Art Museum, though he has lived in the south of France for many years. Orn Þosteinsson and Steinunn Þórurinsdóttir are both successful full-time sculptors, while Rafn Sigurbjörnsson and Páll

Modern art is part of the backdrop to the city of Reykjavík

Stefánsson are leading landscape photographers. A visit to the various buildings that compose the Reykjavík Art Museum (*see pp47–8*) will give you an insight into their work.

Theatre

Despite its small population, Iceland supports two major professional theatre companies (the Reykjavík National Theatre and the City Theatre) and both perform works written by native playwrights including Sigurður Pálsson, Bjarni Jónsson, Ólafur Haukur Símonarson, Þorunn Sigurðardóttir and Sveinn Einarsson.

Major novels by writers such as Laxness have also been transformed into stage plays since the 1990s. Iceland's theatre is probably the most difficult area of the arts for non-Icelandic speakers to access, because of the language barrier.

The worlds of theatre and film (*see p26*) are merging more and more, with many writers, directors and actors actively working in both genres. Dance lovers can enjoy performances by the Icelandic Dance Company.

Music

Since the start of the 1980s, Iceland has been a hotspot in the world of popular

Culture

ICELAND AT THE MULTIPLEX

Iceland can be spotted in the following blockbuster Hollywood films: James Bond's *Die Another Day*, *Lara Croft: Tomb Raider*, *Batman Begins* and *Flags of Our Fathers*. Filming in Iceland is popular, not least because of the 20 per cent refund of production costs by the country's film industry and the long, light summer nights ensuring long shoots. Jökulsárlón, an iceberg-filled lagoon in southern Iceland, is a huge cinematic hit.

music, led by, but by no means limited to, the unique musical phenomenon that is Björk.

Björk released her first album in 1976 at the age of 11 and only a few years later took to punk like a duck to water. The band she fronted, the Sugarcubes, exploded on to the international scene in the late 1980s. Later she embarked upon a successful solo career but throughout has retained her inimitable and indefinable perspective on music and the world.

But this writer/musician/performer did not emerge from a musical vacuum. A generation of young Icelandic musicians had laid the bedrock of today's vibrant scene, creating a network of interconnecting bands with a reputation for expanding the envelope. The five-day music festival in Reykjavík, Iceland Airwaves, celebrates the best local bands and cutting-edge new music from around the world each October. The Icelandic cultural scene certainly is not about being pigeonholed.

The momentum continues with bands like the ethereal Sigur Rós, who have had sustained success with their 'hopelandic' ballads and film scores. Also worth keeping an ear out for are Hjaltalin, Retro Stefson, Agent Fresco and FM Belfast, who make regular appearances in London's hippest clubs. Jónsi, the lead singer of Sigur Rós, has also had success with his solo material.

Film

There was no film industry in Iceland until the late 1980s, but in a few years since then a small band of directors and their often inexperienced cast and crew have taken the world of cinema by storm. The founding father of the industry is Fridrik Thór Fridriksson whose energies led to the founding of the Icelandic Film Corporation in 1987; the same year, the government approved the creation of the Cinema Foundation. Icelandic film made it into the big time when the Fridriksson-directed *Children of Nature* was nominated for an Oscar in the best foreign film category in 1991.

Today, Iceland's films lean towards pseudo-documentary, telling the story of fettered and frustrated youth in a socially fragmented modern society. Some of the best include *101 Reykjavík* by Baltasar Kormákur (2000), *Nói Albinói* by Dagur Kári (2002) and Ágúst Godmundsson's *The Seagull's Laughter* (2001). Kormákur's *Jar City*, a Reykjavík crime drama, had an international release in 2006. A sequel is planned.

Sólfar, the Sun Voyager, is a sculpture based on the skeleton of a Viking ship in Reykjavík

The Icelandic *Eddas* and *Sagas*

The single most important source of information about Iceland's history and the central element of Iceland's national psyche, the *Sagas* are a unique series of epic accounts relating the history of the original Viking settlers penned by later Christian chroniclers directly from an earlier oral tradition.

Over 40 *Sagas* were written. They give us a blow-by-blow account of

Saga writer Snorri Sturluson, immortalised in wax in the Saga Museum

Icelandic society from its first fledgling agreements through to the collapse of the rule of law. They are also filled with wonderfully intimate details of love affairs, family feuds, births and deaths as the generations passed. They are not just dry records but rich chronicles of daily life.

Most of the *Sagas* were written anonymously but the younger *Edda and Heimskringla* – a book about the lives of the Norwegian monarchy – was written by Snorri Sturluson, a celebrated writer in his own time.

The *Eddas*

Eddas differ from the *Sagas* in that they relate to the Norse mythology with epic tales of the old pagan gods (*see pp70–71*). Though the *Sagas* do contain a mythological element, they deal mainly with human relations.

Why were they written?

Saga specialist Arni Björnsson feels that the answer lies in the unique structure of early Icelandic society. With no monarchy and no hereditary aristocracy, the most important people in society were independent farmers, rich and poor. Perhaps these farmers wanted to preserve their

everyone has knowledge of the first settlers/heroes almost from day one and they are still bestsellers in their native land.

Snorri Sturluson

The life of the most famous *Saga* writer, Snorri, reads like a *Saga* itself. Born in Hvamm in western Iceland in 1179 into an influential landowning family, he followed in his father's footsteps and became a *goðar*, or local leader, with many tracts of land. In 1215, he was elected as *Lögsöumaður* (see p18) and a couple of years later he travelled to Norway to meet King Hákon Hákonarson, for whom he wrote an epic poem.

Snorri lived in a time, now known as the Sturlung Age, when Icelandic society was imploding. The writer and his family were in the thick of the action. Snorri fell from royal approval and a rival nephew became the king's favourite. When things got ugly Snorri went into exile in Norway, but when his nephew was killed he thought it safe to return to Iceland despite a royal decree banning him. King Hákon decreed that Snorri return to Norway or face death but Hákon's agent in Iceland, Gisor Thorvaldsson, who was building a power base for himself, did not offer him an option. On 23 September 1241, a gang of men arrived at Snorri's farm and he was brutally killed.

An illuminated manuscript

history as a way of celebrating their success in building a new nation.

The *Sagas* today

Today, many historians view the *Sagas* as important historical texts, although they recognise that they contain romanticised elements. Archaeologists found traces of a settlement at L'Anse aux Meadows in Newfoundland that *Saga* texts would suggest are of Viking origin. The *Sagas* feature in the curriculum of all primary schools in Iceland so

Festivals and events

Iceland has a whole host of festivals, many going back to its Viking and pagan ancestry but also some remarkably modern and 21st-century ones. The arts scene is very busy in the short summer season.

Icelanders enjoy letting their hair down and national celebrations usually involve imbibing large amounts of alcohol. However, the high spirits rarely spill over into drunken behaviour.

January–February
Þrettándinn – the 13th day after Christmas is celebrated with bonfires, fireworks and songs.

Bóndadagur – also known as Husbands Day, when wives and girlfriends serve up rams' testicles and sheep's head to their partners (19 January).

Þorrablót – Iceland's midwinter feast is a traditional event where people gather to sing, drink and eat traditional Icelandic food like *hákarl* (putrefied shark), *blóðmör* (filled sausage/black pudding), *svið* (jellied sheep's head) and other preserved winter food (22 January–21 February).

February
Winter Lights Festival – a three-day event in Reykjavík with diverse cultural happenings around town.

Food and Fun Festival – top foreign chefs convene for five days to create special menus in Reykjavík's top restaurants (late February).

February–March
Buns Day – the Monday before Ash Wednesday is celebrated with the consumption of pastries filled with jam and cream. Children decorate special 'bun wands' and wake early to torment their parents with them.

Bursting Day – the Tuesday before Ash Wednesday has Icelanders eating salted meat and peas until they 'burst'.

Ash Wednesday – on the seventh Wednesday before Easter, children dress in costumes and tour the towns singing in return for sweets.

March–April
Beer Day is on 1 March, celebrating the day when beer was legalised back in 1989.

Holy Thursday marks the start of the Easter holidays for Icelanders, who enjoy a five-day 'weekend'.

The First Day of Summer is a day of festivities as people emerge from a winter of almost total darkness (the first Thursday after 18 April).

Late May–early June
Reykjavík Arts Festival – a two-week
gathering of native and international
cultural events from art to opera.

June–July
Iceland's longest days are celebrated
with all-night parties, walks and hikes.
Festival of the Sea has cultural events
and parades (first weekend).
National Day witnesses celebrations
around the country (17 June).
Summer Solstice – 21 June is the
longest day of the year. Celebrations are
held throughout the country.
Arctic Open – a golf tournament that
invites competitors to tee off under
the midnight sun (late June).
Landsmót Horse Festival brings the
equine community together in a
biennial event (late June–early July).

July–August
Akureyri Arts Festival is celebrated
with plays, concerts and exhibitions
(all month–late August).
Summer concerts – Skálholt Cathedral
complex (mid-July–mid-August).

August
Flight of the Puffling – early August, in
the Westman Islands, sees millions of
baby puffins leave their nests for the
first time (see pp129–30).
Bank Holiday Weekend – various
events and festivities mark the long
weekend (first weekend).
Gay Pride sees a day of parades and
open-air concerts (second weekend).

Reykjavík Culture Night – free
concerts and other activities (third
weekend) (see p157).
Reykjavík Marathon – the city gives
itself over to serious and fun runners.
An average of 3,500 people take part,
including around 500 foreign
competitors (third weekend).
Festival of Sacred Arts, Hallgrímskirkja
– classical performances by international
artists, choirs and orchestras (late
August, biennially on odd years).

September
The Reykjavík Film Festival, Jazz
Festival and Dance Festival (see p154)
take place in the capital.
Réttir – all the sheep and horses that
have been free-grazing around the
island are rounded up.

October
Iceland Airwaves Festival – this five-
day musical event brings local and
international music groups to small
venues around Reykjavík (see p26).

December
Winter Solstice – on 21 December, the
shortest day of the year.
Þorláksmessa – on 23 December, when
a tribute is paid to one of Iceland's few
indigenous saints, St Þorlákur.
Christmas preparations reach a high
point and shops are open until 11pm.
New Year's Eve – on 31 December,
Icelanders say goodbye to the old year
with an enormous fireworks display in
and around the capital at midnight.

Impressions

*Iceland is Europe's northwesternmost country, set jus[t]
below the Arctic Circle and surrounded by the cold water[s]
of the Atlantic Ocean. It is the most sparsely populate[d]
country on the Continent and its wide open spaces can b[e]
reached by a three-hour flight from mainland Europe or i[n]
just over five hours from northeastern USA.*

When to go

More than most other destinations on the planet it is important to pick the right season to visit to get the most out of Iceland.

The 'Land of the Midnight Sun' has days of widely differing lengths, with long days in summer and short, almost totally dark days in winter.

The year-round sunrise and sunset times in Reykjavík are given below – in towns further north, days are longer in summer and shorter in winter.

The 21-hour summer days and 5-hour winter days make a big seasonal difference to the atmosphere of the island. Summer is packed with festivals and events, fun runs and sporting contests, and there is a very jovial atmosphere. Locals are outdoors walking and hiking in the national parks and in the highlands, camping, fishing and getting back to their roots.

The 'tourist' season runs from June to early September. This is not only because the days are longest at this time. It is also because university and high-school students on holiday are free to take up the slack as hotel waiters, hotel-room cleaners, museum or outdoor-pursuits guides. Summer is also the safest and surest time to visit Iceland's hinterland. The roads are open (usually from late May to mid-September depending on the weather) and in the best condition.

All this does not mean that you should not visit outside this period. Iceland has much to offer in every season, especially if you have specialist interests.

Date	Sunrise	Sunset
January 1	11.19	15.45
February 1	10.07	17.16
March 1	08.35	18.47
April 1	06.45	20.20
May 1	04.59	21.52
June 1	03.22	23.31
July 1	03.05	23.57
August 1	04.34	22.31
September 1	06.10	20.43
October 1	07.36	18.57
November 1	09.11	17.11
December 1	10.46	15.48

The island benefits from the warm currents of the Gulf Stream that force warm air northward, tempering the fiercest Arctic temperatures. The weather can be clement through spring and autumn and on a sunny winter's day the island looks magical, though the interior is off-limits to all but specialist vehicles.

Many of Iceland's major attractions are accessible throughout the year – they don't turn off the Strokkur geyser in September – and some of its activities, including quad biking, are better when there is snow on the ground. The island's fledgling ski industry has facilities for the sport under floodlight, so even when the daylight is short, the time on the piste is longer than that in, say, the Alps, Dolomites or Pyrenees.

Reykjavík is a year-round destination and looks particularly beautiful with a covering of snow on a crisp winter's day. The city's residents are used to the cold and dark, and the weekly pub-crawl carries on whatever the weather conditions.

What to wear

There is a motto in Iceland: if you don't like the weather wait for five minutes because it is bound to change. Many visitors have experienced four seasons in one day.

Iceland's weather can and does change frequently. You can get cold spells in summer and rain at all times of the year. Global warming is also increasingly apparent as summers are getting warmer and winters milder, so

Impressions

The ice seems to glow as dawn breaks over the Eyjafjallajökull glacier

From November to April, the spectacular aurora borealis are visible across Iceland

the motto is 'be prepared', and carry warm and waterproof clothing no matter what time of year you travel. Layering is advisable so that you can add or take off a layer of clothing. Breathable lightweight fabrics are ideal for the climate; microfibre fleeces are a good idea as they will add little weight to your luggage but provide good insulation. A good weatherproof jacket is a must, along with comfortable shoes for city walking and rugged shoes for the rest of the country – lava flows and volcanic rock can wreak havoc on shoe-soles, and uneven surfaces mean that you need good ankle support. Don't forget to pack swimming costumes for the natural pools, whatever the weather.

If you are travelling in a hire car, carry warm clothing with you in case of emergency.

Getting around

The last 40 years have seen tremendous development in transport links. The main ring road around the island was completed in 1974, allowing easy access for the first time to the northeast region across the *sandur* volcanic desert. Since then, the asphalting of roads has continued apace. The huge progress in motor-vehicle technology over the last 20 or so years has made a big difference to getting around. Power steering, 4WD and ABS have made driving safer for self-driven vehicles, buses and tour vehicles. GPS navigation systems have also made travel in the highlands safer – many hire cars come with them, too.

Driving yourself is the only way to get to Iceland's most remote attractions. But it is still possible to enjoy a cross-section of what the country has to offer without a car. You can take one of the many day or multiple-day tours organised by Reykjavík Excursions or Iceland Excursions. These have been specifically designed to showcase the best of Iceland's landscape and culture.

Or, there are cross-country buses that link all the major towns. Contact *www.trex.is* for details of multi-destination passes. In summer, buses even run over the highland road through the heart of the country. However, journey times may be long and connections are not always seamlessly planned.

The other option is to take an internal flight. Planes from the airport in the heart of Reykjavík (for more details, see *www.airiceland.is*) fly to a range of Icelandic towns (most internal flights last less than an hour), and you can pick up a hire car or get on to a tour bus once you have reached your destination. Prices are cheaper via the Internet.

Culture shock

The following thoughts are a truly non-scientific listing of the idiosyncrasies of Iceland. They are in no particular order but simply offer a flavour of the national psyche.

The midday moon glows over Perlan, Reykjavík, in winter

Iceland has many beautiful beaches

(bathing in a pool fed by geothermically heated water) and holding raucous midnight parties. But, conversely, it is also the land of the lunchtime moon and research has proved that long periods of darkness can contribute to 'seasonal affective disorder', or, in the form of the most appropriate acronym, SAD. It is difficult to maintain one's equilibrium in winter and a percentage of the population does suffer from depression. For some, heavy drinking is the way to get through the winter despite the high price of alcohol.

Trolls

In a recent survey, most Icelanders said they believed in trolls. These naughty little rascals wreak havoc across the island causing cars to break down, plumbing to go haywire and traffic to snarl up just when you want to catch that transport connection. Some Icelanders think the trolls were stowaways aboard Viking ships during the very first days of settlement, and that they loved this remote landscape so much that they inhabited all the little nooks and crannies on the coast and in the hills. Your best bet to avoid their effect on your trip is to think happy Zen thoughts as the creatures are believed to thrive on negativity!

What's in a name?

Icelanders have worked for centuries on a patronymic name system. There are no family names but the name trail shows

Irreverence

Icelanders have a mischievous and sarcastic sense of humour and a forthright approach once you have broken the ice with them. They hold little truck with power, authority or small talk. Expect to be surprised by the way conversations turn deep and meaningful within minutes of your meeting an Icelander.

People of the Midnight Sun?

We have already mentioned that Iceland is the Land of the Midnight Sun and its citizens, especially those living in Reykjavík, make the most of the long days by camping, hiking, hotpotting

the lineage of each family through the generations. Children take a given first name, then the father's first name followed by either *sson* (meaning 'son of') or *sdóttir* (meaning 'daughter of'). When women marry they don't take their husband's name. So a family of four – father, mother, son and daughter – will all have different last names.

As an example, if Sigrun and Jón have a girl and a boy called Döra and Árnar, the little girl will be known as Döra Jónsdóttir while the little boy will be called Árnar Jónsson. When Árnar grows up to have his own son called Leifur, the child will be known as Leifur Árnarsson.

Because of this unique system, Icelanders have never developed a formal approach to social interaction, and nearly everyone has a nickname to avoid confusion by the duplication of names, e.g. Palli for Pall, Sigga for Sigrun. People call each other by their first names no matter what their social relations. The only people to have formal titles are the president and the bishop of Iceland (and even then the president is referred to as 'the president of Iceland Ólafur Ragnar Grímsson', not as 'President Grímsson'). The egalitarian first-names-only approach of Icelanders is exceptionally refreshing.

A flock of terns hover over the lake near Bessastaðir, the Icelandic president's residence

Take a look in an Icelandic phone directory and you will find people are listed by their given names!

There is also a unique website that lets Icelanders look up their ancestors through an extensive tracing system.

A fantastic set of wheels

Without doubt, one of the most exciting and interesting parts of your visit to Iceland will be the driving. Away from the main asphalted roads are hundreds of kilometres of compacted dirt roads that make you feel like you are on some kind of a pioneering expedition. And after a couple of days on the road, you will notice that you are developing a whole new mindset as far as motor vehicles are concerned.

You will start by noticing a little twinge of envy for the guy in the truck sporting super-sized tyres that passes you on the road. You will find yourself stopping in the street to admire little accessories on the exterior like roof spotlights and tow hooks. The longer you are on the island, the more alluring the big Arctic trucks, with the ultimate in off-road modifications, will become. Call it some kind of hypnotic effect – or maybe it is the strong landscape – that brings out the macho rally driver in all of us.

A lingering aftertaste

Icelanders have been brought up on the adage that a dose of cod liver oil (*lýsi*) a day will keep you fit and healthy, and it is certainly true that the vitamin D in

the oil compensates for what they don't get from sunlight during the winter.

Being generous folk, they occasionally put out a bottle of the oil at the breakfast table in hotels and guesthouses so that you, too, can take a tot every morning. It is wise to remember, though, that this cod liver oil is not the type sanitised for the rest of the world. Iceland's cod liver oil smells and tastes fishy.

Boarding schools

If you were wondering about schooling, children from remote farmsteads are used to leaving home for boarding school during term-time. This is another reason why Icelanders are confident and self-reliant – because they leave the nest so early. Most schools are so modern and comfortable that they double up as hotels during the summer holidays.

Whaling

Icelanders have made a living from commercial whaling for centuries, and hunting has supplemented their meagre diet in this harsh environment. Today, the attitudes towards both activities may have changed around the world but many Icelanders still regard them as legitimate.

This is one country where you will be able to hear a coherent and structured argument in favour of whaling and hunting, although most people under 25 are not accustomed to eating whale nor inclined to take up the habit. The

Whaling boats in Reykjavík's old harbour

main line of reasoning is that the sea in this part of the world is teeming with whales and the limited numbers hunted each year won't affect the population numbers. In 2010, Iceland threatened to withdraw from the International Whaling Commission (IWC) if it was restricted any further. The sport is highly profitable but is damaging to the tourist industry.

Prices and affordability
Up until Iceland's currency crash in 2008, the country was perceived as highly expensive with prices comparable to those in Tokyo and Oslo. Not any more. From 2010, the country has been dubbed a 'value' destination – it's not cheap but it has never been so inexpensive. Prices compare to capital cities like London; remember that much has to be imported so it does cost more than you'd expect.

Tourism is erupting
The very newest attraction for thrill-seekers in Iceland is the sport of volcano-watching. Following the eruption of a small volcano under Eyjafjallajökull glacier in spring 2010, it is expected that the next few years will bring more of the same. Historically, every time this volcano has erupted, it has triggered a much larger eruption of the Katla volcano nearby and lava has flowed for the following few years. Helicopter rides over the crater and 4WD tours are popular ways to see it.

Reykjavík

In the southwest of the country, sitting on the edge of the Faxaflói Bay, Reykjavík's position was determined by a superstitious Viking back in AD 874. Today, Reykjavík's colourful collection of corrugated-iron-clad houses still makes it look more like a village than a capital city but don't be fooled. It has an outsized reputation for partying and is defiantly metropolitan, at the forefront of technology and design.

Reykjavík has plenty to offer all the year round. It is a friendly city where you can walk between attractions, and cultural tourism can be interspersed with a coffee or something stronger at one of numerous atmospheric café/bars where you can rest weary feet. As day turns into night the bars and clubs – from techno to hard rock – come into their own, especially at weekends, as an army of revellers stroll from establishment to establishment. The *runtur*, as it is known, has become legendary in the clubbing world.

Fjölskyldu-og húsdýragarðurinn (Reykjavík Zoo and Family Park)

At the heart of the park is Reykjavík Zoo, with the only live animal collection on the island. Don't expect to see any exotic species as most would not be very happy in Iceland's climate. Instead, this is the perfect place to find native species, many of which can rarely be seen in the wild because they inhabit the most remote corners of the island. You will find Arctic foxes and reindeer here, as well as domestic species such as horses and cattle, plus the sheep that are too skittish to approach in the wild. The zoo serves as a rehabilitation centre for birds and animals before they are re-released into the wild. There is also an aquarium with North Atlantic fish species as well as Science World, where you can enjoy various interactive exhibits such as measuring how loud you can scream or blowing huge soap bubbles.

Laugardalur (see p43), 104 Reykjavík. Tel: 411 5900. www.mu.is

REYKJAVÍK WELCOME CARD

The Reykjavík Welcome Card offers entrance to a number of museums and attractions including the thermal pools in the city, along with free public transport and free Internet access at the tourist office. There are also discounts on some tours. Cards are valid for 24, 48 or 72 hours, and can be bought from tourist information offices and some hotels. For more information, visit the city website (*www.visitreykjavik.is*).

For the walk route, see pp44–5

Reykjavik

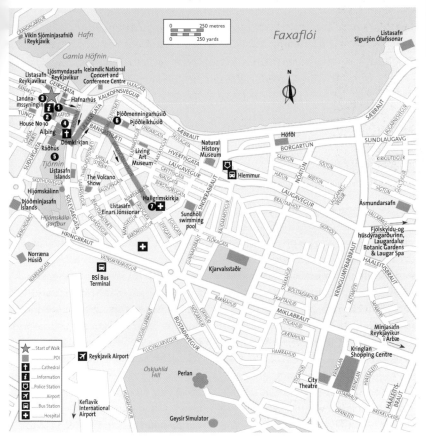

*Open: summer daily 10am–6pm; winter daily 10am–5pm. Admission charge.
Bus: 2, 14 and 15.*

Gamla Höfnin (Old Harbour)

The capital still has a fishing fleet and there is an air of gritty workaday reality at the port, although most boats bring their catch into the new harbour, opposite Viðey Island. Come down to the old harbour to take

advantage of the whale- or puffin-watching trips that depart daily (weather permitting) and trips out to Viðey Island (*see pp54–5*).

Hallgrímskirkja (Hallgríms Church)

The towering stark white outline of Iceland's tallest building can be seen from all around the surrounding countryside. Commissioned in 1937, the church took 38 years to build. Its elegantly expansive façade was designed to resemble one of Iceland's most evocative landscapes, the sheer face of a glacier or ice flow. Unusually, the church was named after a clergyman, Reverend Hallgrímur Pétursson, who wrote some of Iceland's finest hymns. The interior of the church is worth a visit, especially to hear a concert on the impressive pipe organ. A trip to the top of the 75m (246ft) steeple is a must for the fantastic views across the city, accessible by lift and stairs.

In the square in front of the church is a magnificent heroic statue of Leifur Eiríksson, the discoverer of Vinland (now thought to be North America). It was presented to the Icelandic people by the USA to mark the 1,000-year anniversary of the founding of the Alþing.
Skólavörðuholti, 101 Reykjavík.
Tel: 510 1000. http://hallgrimskirkja.is.

Hallgrímskirkja

Open: daily 9am–5pm. Tower open: daily 9am–5pm. Service Sun 11am. Admission charge for tower.

Höfði

Set overlooking the Reykjavík shoreline, this early 1900s catalogue house ordered from Norway from the French consul has a rather spectacular history. During World War II, Winston Churchill and Marlene Dietrich both stayed here (though, I hasten to add, not together) and it became the seat of British diplomacy after the war. The British ambassador swore the house was haunted and it was sold. It later came into the hands of the municipality of Reykjavík, who used it as a reception venue. It has seen presidents, queens and other heads of state but its finest moment was in 1986 when it hosted the historic Reagan–Gorbachev summit that saw the beginning of the end of the Cold War.
Borgartún. Closed to public.

Landnamssyningin (The Settlement Exhibition, Reykjavík 871±2)

This archaeological site was discovered in 2001. Once excavation had begun, the hotel that was scheduled to open on the site actually built around the ruins, which are now housed in a structure below, with extensive exhibition space enhanced by a range of multimedia. Various methods are employed to explain and interpret the remains of the building, and in a reconstruction

Laugar Spa, in Reykjavík, is popular with all the family

window there are controls for calling up three-dimensional imagery of how the hall may have looked. On the multimedia table is a large model of the hall, with diverse information on the archaeologists' research findings and methods, the hall as it was, and the life and work that went on there. Two touch-screens give information about cultural affinities between different North Atlantic nations and how the Vikings settled in new countries. The museum shop has a unique selection of T-shirts and souvenirs.

Aðalstræti 16. Tel: 411 6370. www.minjasafnreykjavíkur.is. Open: daily 10am–5pm. Audio tours available in English. Admission charge.

Laugardalur

The largest green space in the city is a magnet for families in the long summer evenings and on sunny weekends throughout the year. The zoo (*see p40*) is the major attraction here but you can spend time enjoying other activities as well. The **Botanic Gardens** have over 5,000 plant species, a woodland garden, rhododendrons (best in May) and a greenhouse containing 130 foreign species.

Close by, Laugar Spa (*see p146*) is the biggest in the city. It's a fully modernised five-star health spa, gym, and swimming pools using the natural hot springs. There are seven hot tubs, an Olympic-sized indoor pool and an outdoor thermal pool.

Botanic Gardens: Skúlatún 2, 105 Reykjavík. Tel: 553 8870. Gardens always open. Café Flora open: Apr–Sept daily 10am–10pm; Oct–Mar daily 10am–5pm. Free admission.

Walk: Reykjavík

The best way to experience central Reykjavík is on foot and in a half-day tour you can get to see several attractions, pacing yourself with regular stops for refreshment and lunch. (The route is marked in orange on the Reykjavík map, p41.)

Time: 4 hours with attraction visits.

Distance: 2.5km (1½ miles).

Start out at the Reykjavík Tourist Information Centre at Aðalstræti 2, where you can pick up background information and a Welcome Card.

1 Faxaflói

The small square in front of the Tourist Information Centre is the heart of the city. Look for a sculpture of tall concrete stakes, running water and steaming plumes. This installation emulates the founding of the city when Ingólfur Arnarson cast the wooden pillars he had brought from Norway into the sea, stating that he would settle wherever they landed. They came to rest in this 'steamy' or 'smoky' bay in the Faxaflói.

Turn right out of the Tourist Information Centre door and walk down Aðalstræti. Just a short distance along, you will come to No 10.

2 House No 10

This is considered to be the oldest wooden house in central Reykjavík and

has been transformed (on the interior) into a centre for Icelandic craft and design, Kraum (*see p151*).

Continue a few doors down Aðalstræti to No 16 where you will come to the Hotel Reykjavík Centrum. Walk to the left of the hotel to access the Settlement Exhibition.

3 Landnamssyningin (The Settlement Exhibition, Reykjavík 871±2)

The exhibition is based on scholars' theories concerning what the heritage sites in central Reykjavík can tell us about the life and work of the first settlers. The focus of the exhibition are the remains of a hall from the Settlement Age which was excavated in 2001. The hall was inhabited in 930–1000. North of the hall are two pieces of turf, remnants of wall which was clearly built shortly before 871. This is one of the oldest man-made structures so far found in Iceland. Also on display are objects from the Viking

Age found in central Reykjavík and on the island of Viðey. It is a fascinating glimpse at Iceland's rich history. *Now cross the street and walk up Austurstræti till you come to a small green park and square.*

4 The Square

The square is graced with a statue of Jón Sigurðsson (1811–79), the father of Icelandic nationalism, while at the far flank is the Alþing (Parliament), a curious amalgam of 18th-century stone and 20th-century glass buildings.

This is still a major gathering spot for demonstrations, outdoor exhibitions and sunbathing in good weather. *Walk down the narrow alleyway to the right of the Parliament and cross Vonarstræti to reach Tjörnin.*

5 Tjörnin

Reykjavík's beautiful lake is always full of birds so carry some breadcrumbs to feed them. You can then make up your own mind as to whether the sleek lines of the Ráðhús (City Hall) enhance or detract from the chocolate-box wooden period homes in various colours that are its close neighbours. *From the eastern corner of Tjörnin (the other end of Vonarstræti from Ráðhús), turn left and walk down Lækjargata. You will re-cross Austurstræti and on your right you will see a long white wooden building, the offices of Iceland's prime minister. Cross Lækjargata at the traffic lights here, turn right and then left on Hverfisgata where you will find*

Þjóðmenningarhúsið (Culture House) about 50m (164ft) up on the left.

6 Þjóðmenningarhúsið (Culture House)

Enjoy the magnificent medieval manuscripts and learn more about Iceland's *Eddas* and *Sagas.*

From Þjóðmenningarhúsið, cross over Hverfisgata, walk right, then left down Ingólfstræti past the Opera House, to Laugavegur, Reykjavík's main shopping street. Turn left here, then right on Skolavörðustigur, the arts district of the city, and walk uphill to Hallgrímskirkja.

7 Hallgrímskirkja

Have your photograph taken in front of Leifur Eiríksson's statue before heading up the church steeple for panoramic views over the city, then stop for a coffee on Skolavörðustigur.

Feed the birds on Tjörnin, Reykjavík's central lake

Listasafn Einars Jónssonar (Einar Jónsson Museum)

This rather austere building hidden behind trees opposite Hallgríms Church was in fact Iceland's first art gallery when it opened in 1923. Designed by sculptor Einar Jónsson in the Art Nouveau style that was so fashionable at the time, the museum displays over 300 of his sculptures and paintings spanning a career of 60 years. The garden contains 26 bronze castings of Einar's works.

Eiriksgata, 101 Reykjavík. Tel: 551 3797. www.skulptur.is. Open: Jun–mid-Sept Tue–Sun 2–5pm; mid-Sept–Nov & Feb–May Sat–Sun 2–5pm. Closed: Dec & Jan. Admission charge.

Listasafn Íslands (National Gallery of Iceland)

The National Gallery's collection comprises leading Icelandic art of the 19th and 20th centuries. Showcasing key works from each genre and artist and maintaining a huge reference library, it is the island's most important repository of art.

When it was founded in 1885 the collection mainly comprised pieces by Danish artists. It was not until 1902 that the first piece by an Icelandic artist – *Outlaws* by Einar Jónsson – was added to the catalogue. Today, the gallery houses over 10,000 works in the permanent home it has had since 1987 (an old freezing plant built in 1916 and restored to a modern structure with glass and white walls), after relocating from the Parliament Building. The gallery offers changing exhibitions, charting artistic genres featuring such early 20th-century Icelandic masters as Thorarinn B Thórláksson, Jóhannes Kjarval, Jón Stefánsson and Nina Tryggvadóttir through to the more

The National Gallery of Iceland

Ásmundarsafn
(Ásmundur Sveinsson Museum)

Ásmundur Sveinsson was one of the most important sculptors of the 20th century and this museum – the artist's self-designed, rather futuristic home and studio from 1942 to 1950 – features over 300 of his modernist sculptures, plus 2,400 sketches, drawings and watercolours. The gardens display over 30 of his monumental pieces.
Sigtún, 105 Reykjavík. Tel: 553 2155. Bus: 2, 14 and 15.

Hafnarhús (Harbour House)

The museum's most cutting-edge gallery is housed in an old warehouse that used to belong to the harbour authority. It is basically a series of six vast connected multi-purpose spaces, some of which are offered as work space to artists. Other areas host regular temporary art exhibitions, concerts and lectures, while the permanent collection includes a large donation by the artist Erró (1932–). The works include paintings, graphics and sculpture from throughout his modernist career.
Tryggvagata 17, 101 Reykjavík. Tel: 590 1200.

The unique artistic style of Ásmundur Sveinsson

contemporary works of Ólafur Elíasson and Ragna Róbertsdóttir. The small international collection includes works by Picasso and Munch. The gift shop is excellent, as is the café.
Fríkirkjuvegi 7, 101 Reykjavík. Tel: 515 9600. Open: Tue–Sun 11am–5pm. Free admission. Bus: 1, 3, 4, 5, 6, 11, 12, 13 and 14.

Listasafn Reykjavíkur (Reykjavík Art Museum)

The Reykjavík Art Museum, through three sites around the city, offers a diverse perspective of art in Iceland.
www.artmuseum.is. Open: Fri–Wed 10am–5pm, Thur 10am–10pm. Free admission.

CITY TOUR

Sightseeing buses run a hop-on, hop-off service through the heart of Reykjavík *Jun–Aug 10am–4pm*, with recorded commentaries in eight languages. Tickets are valid for 24 hours and the route takes 60 minutes in full. For more details, *tel: 580 5400. www.city-sightseeing.com*

An overview of the city

Listasafn Sigurjón Ólafssonar (Sigurjón Ólafsson Museum)

Ólafsson was a contemporary of Sveinsson (*see pp24–5 & p47*) but worked in many more media than Sveinsson. He moved between the surreal and realistic genres, spanning many of the important developments in art during the 20th century. The museum is housed in his old studio set on Reykjavík's seafront and displays works by the artist in wood, metal, stone and clay, plus a selection of works by other sculptors.

Laugernastangi, 105 Reykjavík.
Tel: 553 2906. www.lso.is. Open:
Jun–Sept Tue–Sun 2–5pm; Oct–Nov &
Feb–May Sat–Sun 2–5pm.
Closed: Dec & Jan. Admission charge.
Bus: 5 and 12.

Kjarvalsstaðir

Inaugurated as a specialist art exhibition hall in 1973, this gallery was named after Jóhannes Sveinsson Kjarval (1885–1972), whose career is intertwined with the rise of Icelandic nationalism in the 20th century, when his romantic landscapes inspired his fellow countrymen. Kjarval donated a selection of his work and many personal items to the city, and these form the permanent collection here – though the works on display change regularly. But Kjarvalsstaðir's main focus is temporary exhibitions featuring the best of Icelandic and international modern art.
Flókagata, 105 Reykjavík. Tel: 517 1290.
Bus: 11 and 13.

Ljósmyndasafn Reykjavíkur (Reykjavík Museum of Photography)

This small museum on the top floor of the city library, by the Hafnarhús and old harbour, has occasional small exhibitions by local photographers as well as a large archive of Icelandic photographs. Themed shows from the archives are often on display and you can buy archive photographs in the museum shop. The museum holds several exhibitions a year.
Tryggvagata 15, 101 Reykjavík.
Tel: 411 6390.
www.ljosmyndasafnreykjavikur.is.
Free admission. Bus: 1, 3, 6, 12
and 14.

Minjasafn Reykjavíkur (í Arbæ – Reykjavík City Museum)

This open-air museum harks back to the Reykjavík of 100 years ago. More than 20 wooden buildings have been carefully renovated in period style to form a town square, farm and village. Many were saved from destruction and brought here from Reykjavík to be installed around the site of the traditional farm of **Árbær** that forms the heart of the museum.

All the buildings here are of architectural merit, even the ticket office, which was built by a stonemason in 1901. Lækjargata 4 (the old address is still used as the name on the site) was the first two-storeyed house in Reykjavík when it was completed in 1852, while the Blacksmith's House (1823) is the oldest house recovered from the central area. The two oldest buildings are the early 1820s warehouses rescued from Vopnafjörður in eastern Iceland that sit by the re-created coastal inlet with its 1930s fishing vessel.

Árbær farm first appeared in the records in the 15th century when it was owned by the religious community on Viðey (*see pp54–5*) before it was taken over by the Danish Crown. The farm changed hands many times but the family of Margrét Pétursdóttir and Eyleifur Einarsson ran it from 1881 until it was finally abandoned in 1948. Many of the farm buildings were erected or expanded during their tenure.

Throughout the summer Árbær is brought alive by a team of costumed guides who live the old country life – farmers tend the land, the ladies spin and weave, and the sailors repair their boats. Old festivals are also re-created so that you can immerse yourself in Icelandic culture. There is also a café and museum shop.

Perlan, once a collection of water-storage tanks, has now been converted into a unique attraction

v/Kistuhyl 4, 110 Reykjavík. Tel: 411
6300. www.minjasafnreykjavikur.is.
Open: Jun–Sept daily 10am–5pm.
Admission charge; valid for two visits
(children are free). Bus: 19.

Norræna Húsið (The Nordic House)

On the far side of the Tjörnin lake,
away from the city, the Nordic House,
designed by Alvar Aalto, is a space
where the Nordic nations come
together. Iceland has strong ties with
Norway, Denmark, Sweden, Greenland,
Finland and the Faroe Islands and this
modernist space is used for cultural
gatherings, concerts, film screenings,
book readings, exhibitions and more.
Its restaurant Dill is one of the most
progressive in the city and the cultural
programme is well worth a look – it's
more left-field and intellectual than any
other you'll find in the city. Even if you
just drop by to admire the architecture,
it's worth it.
Sturlugata 5, 101 Reykjavík. Tel: 551
7030. www.nordice.is.
Admission charge; free Wed.
Bus: 1, 3, 6 and 14.

Perlan (The Pearl)

Perlan is one of Reykjavík's signature
attractions and in many ways it
epitomises the city's offbeat personality.
Once a simple collection of round water
storage tanks on a small hill to the south
of the city centre, Perlan was rescued
from destruction by the vision of one
man who saw more in it than huge
empty tin cans. Today, the tanks have
been capped by a glass roof and the
space inside is multifunctional, being
used for conferences and exhibitions,
and even weddings. One of the city's
most expensive restaurants, Perlan, is
located on the top floor. There is also a
good café. The viewing platform around
the third floor offers panoramic views
over the city and the bay.

The major attraction within Perlan is
the **Saga Museum**, a must for all
interested in Viking history and the
perfect complement to your trip to the
Culture House (see p45 & pp51–2) and
the National Museum of Iceland (see
pp52–3). By means of a guided CD
tour, this museum brings to life the
tales found in those genuine Saga
documents and priceless artefacts.

Almost 20 of the pivotal moments in
Iceland's history are depicted here with
the help of the most lifelike full-size

The Culture House is home to the medieval
manuscripts of the Sagas and Eddas

A Viking boat exhibit in the National Museum of Iceland

silica figures ever produced – Ingólfur Arnarson (the first settler) and Snorri Sturluson are scarily real – and the closest attention to the authenticity of all the objects on display. The graphic details of witch-hunts, battles and beheadings, and the imaginative English commentary that accompanies each of the dioramas are captivating, and you will come away with a greater appreciation of Iceland's history in addition to being entertained. Equally interesting is the documentary film that shows the making of the figures and displays.

Perlan is surrounded by verdant parkland where you can take a stroll in conducive weather or walk down the hill and visit the thermally heated beach at Nautholsvík bay where natural water flows out to the sea. An artificial geyser spouts forth on a regular basis, offering a glimpse of Iceland's natural wonders.

Perlan Öskjuhlið, 105 Reykjavík. Tel: 562 0200. www.perlan.is. Open: Apr–Sept daily 10am–6pm; Oct–Mar daily noon–5pm. Free admission. Saga Museum: tel: 511 1517. www.sagamuseum.is. Admission charge. Bus: 19.

Þjóðmenningarhúsið (The Culture House)

The exhibition at the Culture House helps put Iceland's medieval

WHAT'S ON IN REYKJAVÍK

www.whatson.is is a free monthly booklet that fills you in on activities and gives you pointers for eating and entertainment. There's also good background information on the latest hotspots, concerts and trends in *Grapevine*, the free English-language newspaper produced fortnightly and online at *www.grapevine.is. Iceland Review*, a glossy magazine, has news of new openings plus reviews and in-depth features.

manuscripts in their context as cultural objects. From here, you can go on to view over 15 original medieval manuscripts and books that constitute the backbone of the country's national identity. Most of these documents were shipped to Copenhagen during Danish rule; the first manuscripts were returned to an emotional welcome in 1971 and over 1,800 came back to Iceland during the 1980s and 1990s.

The initial exhibition gallery does a good job of giving the background to the creation of the books including an explanation of the oral tradition during pagan times, how the *Eddas* and *Sagas* were written down when scribes arrived on the island with the coming of Christianity, and how the *Book of Settlement* – charting the development of Iceland's society – came about.

The highlight of the Culture House is without doubt the original manuscripts themselves. Law codices including the *Codex Regius* of Elder Edda and an early translation of the Bible are illuminating but most precious are the original *Saga* manuscripts including *Egils Saga*, the *Book of Settlement* and *Möðruvallabók* – the most important single collection of Icelandic *Sagas* in the world.

In addition, the Culture House is also open for exhibitions of photography and recent art, musical recitals and ceremonies. There is a café and gift shop on the ground floor.
Hverfisgata 15, 101 Reykjavík.
Tel: 545 1400. www.thjodmenning.is.
Open: daily 11am–5pm.
Admission charge; free Wed.

Þjóðminjasafn Íslands (National Museum of Iceland)

The National Museum is an impressive showcase of Iceland's rich and diverse history. Set chronologically, the

A view of the city from Lake Tjörnin

permanent collection leads from the earliest settlers to the present day in a clever combination of artefacts, oral accounts, interactive databases, film and photographic archives. Each section of the museum has a signature piece that somehow defines the larger collection around it, and an Icelandic 'resident' – a personality around whom the folkloric accounts are based.

You are first welcomed into a beautifully designed space devoted to the Viking and Celtic era leading through to the early Christian period, including two pagan burials set into the museum floor just as they were found by archaeologists.

Venture upstairs to continue the journey through the Danish era and into the 20th century. Depictions of the the tribulations of the 17th century include details of the witch trials of the Strandir region (*p81 & pp141–3*), while the 19th century features artefacts of the crofter lifestyle including a small, single-room family home. The most dramatic single object on the second floor is a fully rigged rowing boat in the centre of the room.

Suðurgata 41, 101 Reykjavík.
Tel: 530 2200. www.natmus.is.
Open: May–mid-Sept daily 10am–5pm;
mid-Sept–Apr Tue–Sun 11am–5pm.
Admission charge. Bus: 1, 3, 6, 11, 12
and 14.

Tjörnin/Ráðhús (City Hall)

This large lake in the middle of the city is the place to come for your lunchtime picnic. Despite its urban setting, over 30 species of wild birds make a home here, many of them migratory summer visitors. Tjörnin is flanked by some of Reykjavík's most beautiful period homes, characterised by their ornate gingerbread wooden decorative detail. The rather incongruous gun-metal-grey concrete structure at the lake's northern end is the Ráðhús (City Hall), a controversial design at the time it was approved and still hotly disputed by locals. Visit the interior to find a 3-D visualisation of Iceland and a great-value café.

Ráðhús Vonarstræti. Open: Mon–Fri
8am–7pm, Sat–Sun noon–6pm.
Free admission.

Víkin Sjóminjasafnið í Reykjavík (Reykjavík Maritime Museum)

Its location in the new harbour area gives Reykjavík's museum of fisheries and coastal culture an authentic atmosphere. One of the main exhibitions celebrates the 90th anniversary of the Reykjavík harbour. The coastguard ship *Óðinn* is docked just outside and other boats and ships will be moored in the same dock, changing periodically. Visiting Iceland without learning about its seagoing history is like going to England and avoiding castles. The sea views from the café are great, too.

Grandagarður 8. Tel: 517 9400.
Open: Jun–Sept Tue–Sun 11am–5pm,
guided tours on Óðinn 1pm, 2pm &
3pm; winter months Sat–Sun
1–5pm. Admission charge.

The City Hall

EXCURSIONS FROM THE CAPITAL
Day tours
If you only have a short time in Iceland, a couple of companies run some excellent day tours from the capital to give you a taste of what you will be missing (though they really are not a substitute for a more comprehensive tour and the itinerary is pretty packed, with only limited time at each location). With all companies, you will be picked up and brought back to your hotel.

The most popular tours are the Golden Circle Route taking in Gullfoss, Geysir and Þingvellir (*see p60, p61, pp67–9, p73 & p74*), the Reykjanes Peninsula (*see pp66–7 & pp74–5*), Þórsmörk, which is difficult to get to without a 4WD vehicle, and a trip along the south coast to the *sandur* and Jökulsárlón glacial lake (*see p122*).

The following companies have a good reputation, comfortable vehicles and English-speaking guides:
IE – Iceland Excursions: *Hafnarstræti 20, 101 Reykjavík. Tel: 540 1313. www.icelandexcursions.is*
Reykjavík Excursions: *BSÍ Bus Terminal, 101 Reykjavík. Tel: 580 5400. www.re.is*

Viðey Island
If you want to escape the bustle of the city, head to Viðey Island out in the bay, just a 15-minute boat ride from Reykjavík. An uninhabited island, it was once the site of a monastery and is still regarded as a religious site. Take a

TOURIST INFORMATION

Tourist information about the city can be obtained at *Aðalstræti 2, 101 Reykjavík. Tel: 590 1550. www.visitreykjavík.is*

picnic and simply enjoy the birdlife and the easy walking trails. Or visit the regular art exhibitions held through the summer. Yoko Ono's light installation *Imagine Peace Tower* throws out a dramatic beam of light from 9 October to 8 December each year, with a wishing well inscribed with the words 'Imagine Peace' in 24 languages.

There is a daily ferry from Reykjavík harbour at 10am returning at 1.15pm. Tel: 533 5055. www.videy.com. From mid-June to mid-August ferries run from Sundahöfn harbour at 8.30am, 1pm, 2pm, 3pm, 7pm & 9pm. Last return journey is at 9.15pm. Take bus 5 to Sundahöfn harbour.

Isolated and enchanting Viðey Island is only a 15-minute boat ride from the capital

Around the capital

The region around Reykjavík sees more visitors than any other area of Iceland apart from the capital itself. There are two reasons for this. First, it is an easy drive from the capital for those on a short stay or for those who don't want to move out of a city hotel. Second, the region has many attractions that give a flavour of the country without having to make a full tour of the island.

The two areas closest to Reykjavík are the rolling farmland immediately east of the city where the 'big three' attractions (Gullfoss, Geysir and Þingvellir) can be found – so called because they are among the most visited and are in close proximity to one another – and the Reykjanes Peninsula, just below the capital.

Akranes

The only real reason for visiting Akranes is the **Akranes Museum Centre**, opened in 1959 and housed on the site of an old manor farm, Garðar, that features in the *Sagas* as the home of Irish settlers in the 9th century and Guðný Böðvarsdóttir *c.* 1200. It was a centre of Christianity from the first days of conversion and the parsonage operated until the late 19th century.

Today, the site has a collection of buildings that tell the story of the development of the town from these humble beginnings through to the early 1900s. The oldest wooden house in the town, erected in 1875, was moved here in 2002 to sit alongside an old fish-drying shed, a boathouse and ketch built in Hull (UK) in 1885. Fróðá's house was used by sail- and net-makers in the 1930s. There is an old school house, Geirsstaðir, christened Geirsstaðir University by the locals.

The folk collection is housed in a separate building and is a fascinating and eclectic mixture of artefacts, large and small, charting the development of the town and showing how daily life changed over the centuries, including an unusual display of medical tools and equipment. Incorporated into the whole are some interesting but seemingly unrelated collections: the Land Survey exhibition, which will attract lovers of geography and show developments in the science since records began; the comprehensive show of rocks in Mineral Kingdom; and the Sport in Iceland collection, which gives insight into Akranes' great footballing past as well as a bicycle that was folded into a ball by a famous weightlifter! *Safnasvæðið Á Akranesi (The Akranes Museum Centre): off Graðagrund. Tel: 431 5566. www.museum.is. Open: Jun–Aug daily 10am–5pm; Sept–May daily 1–5pm. Admission charge.*

Bessastaðir

The site of an ancient manor farm less than 10km (6 miles) from central Reykjavík, the complex at Bessastaðir, which is set amid coastal lowland and lava fields, is now the official residence of the president of Iceland, on the Álftanes Peninsula.

First mentioned in the *Íslendinga Saga,* the farm was owned by storyteller Snorri Sturluson (*see pp28–9*); it passed to the Norwegian throne and remained a royal estate until it was bought for a school in 1805. It reverted to a private farm in 1867. The present building is one of the oldest in Iceland, having been erected in 1761. It became the president's official residence in 1941. There is also a small church (1777) and a graveyard on the site.

Church: open to the public daily 9am–5pm except when the president is in residence. House and grounds private property. Free admission.

Around the capital

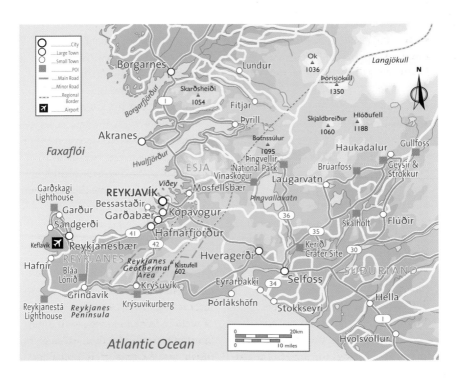

Bláa Lónið (Blue Lagoon)

Probably Iceland's most famous tourist attraction, the Blue Lagoon is a beautiful complex of geothermal pools fed by the continental rift. Perhaps it ruins the romance, but the waters travel through the Svartsengi power plant before they hit the pools – ever practical, the Icelanders! The lagoon is revered for its pools, which are set against a black volcanic basalt backdrop – the whole concept is Caribbean-meets-geothermal springs and it is unique. The waters are also rich in mud that has been proved to be highly beneficial for one's skin. You can spend hours here just lounging in the shallows, taking a massage or sunbathing – yes, it is possible in Iceland. The Lava restaurant has an excellent reputation, so take a break for a long lunch. The waters are not good to precious metals, so leave your jewellery back in your hotel safe for the day.

Whether you go in summer or winter, you're bound to have an unusual experience – surrounded by snow in piping hot water or under the midnight sun. Strategically placed boxes of silica mud are available for DIY facemasks; if you want more than that, book a treatment in advance – they have a wide variety on offer, including in-water massages.

The Blue Lagoon also has a clinic with an award-winning architectural design, specialising in skin treatments. As well as the restaurant, there is a shop, café and bar. If you feel thirsty while you're in the pool, their sophisticated system means you can order a drink to have in the water and pay for it via a wristband.

During Iceland Airwaves Festival in October (*see p31*), the lagoon plays host to visiting bands – so you could enjoy a gig or two from the water. *Blue Lagoon Road, Grindavík. Tel: 420 8800. www.bluelagoon.com. Open: Jun–Aug daily 9am–9pm; Sept–May daily 10am–8pm. Admission charge.*

Enjoy a natural spa treatment at the Blue Lagoon

Eyrarbakki

Once home to the largest community in southwestern Iceland, this small coastal town has a large selection of late 19th- and early 20th-century architecture, plus a couple of important historical

The Garðskagi Lighthouse

landmarks. Húsið and Assistenta Húsið are two connected structures that were ordered from a kit catalogue from Scandinavia. **Húsið** (the House of Merchants) was erected in 1765 and is one of the oldest wooden structures on the island, while Assistenta Húsið was added over a century later, in 1881. Húsið now houses the Húsið Folk Museum with exhibitions about the history of the town and its people.

Eyrarbakki was the home of one of Iceland's greatest Viking explorers, Bjarni Herjólfsson, who sailed west in the 980s and was probably the first European to spot the North American coast. His tales caught the imagination of Leifur Eiríksson, who named this new discovery Vinland.

Húsið. Tel: 483 1504. www.husid.com. Open: mid-May–mid-Sept daily 11am–6pm; mid-Sept–mid-May by arrangement. Admission charge.

Garður

Set on the northernmost point of the Reykjanes Peninsula, Garður is a small village surrounded by some of the best birdwatching landscape on the island, not least from the town museum's new showroom and top-floor café. The Garðskagi Lighthouse erected in 1944 on the site of an earlier *phare* (lighthouse) marks the most northerly point, and is the tallest lighthouse in Iceland.

The **Byggðasafnið á Garðskaga** (Garður Peninsula Historical Museum) tells the story of fishermen and fishing, which was an important industry for many years in many places across the island. Pride of place goes to the engines dating from 1924 to 1977, collected with love and devotion by Guðni Ingimundarson. Garður also has an interesting church, Útskálakirkja, finished in 1863. There is a large

Strokkur at sunset

attempts were made to make the spout gush on command and eventually it stopped completely – it is now little more than a constant steamy emission. A new pretender has taken over the throne, only metres from the last king. Strokkur is every bit its father's son, spouting every 5–7 minutes as high as 15m (49ft) into the air – though the height varies with the strength of the pressure below the surface. Crowds of all ages gather enthralled, waiting for the next expulsion, which is always accompanied by a hiss of steam.

Around the two geyser sites is an area of geothermic activity with fumaroles and hot steamy springs. It is a good introduction to what makes Iceland special in relation to volcanic activity.

outdoor swimming pool in town as well, and a beautiful golf course. *Byggðasafnið á Garðskaga: tel: 422 7108. Open: May–Aug daily 1–5pm; Sept–Apr by arrangement. Admission charge.*

Geysir and Strokkur

The spectacular gush of hot steamy water rising regularly through a small hole in the ground was called 'Geysir' by Icelanders. Eventually, the name became synonymous with a hot-water spout, and Geysir became geyser in the English language. Today, the original Geysir can still be visited, though the 'old man' is well past his prime. Throughout the 20th century, many

Grindavík

A modern fishing town, Grindavík is worth a visit for **Saltfisksetur Íslands** (the Saltfish Museum). This new museum complex explains the development of salting as a means of preserving fish and covers the heyday of salting in the area around the start of the last century. Real saltfish are placed around the exhibition to bring home the smell and sight of the product, and these are complemented by dioramas and photographs that document the processes. You can also enjoy fishy snacks at the café on-site.

The town's main church, Grindavíkurkirkja, was inaugurated in 1982. Only the small cross atop the white-painted water-tower-like steeple indicates that it is a place of worship.

A visit to the municipal pool is welcome after a day spent at the Saltfish Museum, followed by a walk on the outskirts of town to a quaint lighthouse and past remains from old shipwrecks.

The Blue Lagoon (*see p58*) lies within Grindavík municipal boundaries.

Saltfisksetur Íslands: Hafnargata 12a. Tel: 420 1190. www.saltfisksetur.is. Open: daily 11am–6pm. Admission charge.

Gullfoss

Iceland's most visited 'foss' is also its most spectacular. It is an L-shaped waterfall with a curtain cascade of white water and a sheer drop into a narrow fissure that leads a drenching spray and deafening noise in the direction of bystanders.

Gullfoss means 'golden falls' in Icelandic. No one is really sure why it has been given this name. Some say that the sunlight playing on the water gives the spray a golden sheen, which is true enough – but only on a bright day! In winter, curtains of ice form around the still-active falls, changing the scene into a white wonderland.

Open access. Free admission.

Hafnarfjörður

One of Iceland's most important fishing towns, Hafnarfjörður products find their way to tables across the world. It has also been a trading town since the 1300s, thanks to the fine natural harbour that gives Hafnarfjörður its name. Today, the

The *Sea and the Man* monument, near the modern fishing town of Grindavík

The spectacular Gullfoss waterfall

Viking life, whatever time of year you may visit. It hosts Viking banquets with wenches and warriors, *Saga* recitals and hearty singing. You can stay in the comfortable hotel if the mead and ale get the better of you. The rooms are decorated in a low-key Viking ambience.

Byggðasafn Hafnarfjörður (Hafnarfjörður Museum)

This collection of three old wooden houses now forms the town museum. The permanent 'Thus It Was…' exhibition tells the story of the history of the town from its first settlers to the development of the fishing industry. There is a special gallery dedicated to the British sojourn in Iceland. **Sívertsen House**, the oldest of the three houses and home to one of the town's most influential families, is furnished in 19th-century period style. In contrast, **Siggubær's Pakkhúsið**, built in 1902, has displays relating to the life of a working family 100 years later.

The town has an excellent gallery, **Hafnarborg**, that hosts ever-changing exhibitions featuring Icelandic artists. This is yet another venue that has on display the rich modern art of the island.

In addition to Viking lore, Hafnarfjörður is famous for having one of Iceland's largest settlements of elves, dwarves and other mystical creatures. A knowledgeable local named Sibba has organised 'Hidden Worlds' walking tours (1½ hours) on Tuesday and

suburbs of Reykjavík have muscled their way against the boundary, but Hafnarfjörður has a strong civic pride that sets it apart from 'the city' just up the road.

There are a quite a few surprises here, not least the jumble of brightly coloured façades of homes that rise above the harbour. Every year in mid-June the town is invaded by hundreds of 'Vikings' dressed in full regalia for the annual 'Viking Festival' that celebrates all things Norse. It is said that some of these people live their life full time, wearing traditional clothes and celebrating pagan festivals. The **Viking Village** is the centre of festival activities – this wooden pavilion carved with dragons' heads and other symbolic images is the place to taste a bit of

Friday afternoons (*at 2.30pm*) to unique sites around town. A map is included with the fee (*tel: 694 2785*).

The outdoor swimming pool is also worth a visit, just a 5-minute walk up the road from the Viking Village.

Viking Village: Strandgata 55. Tel: 565 1213. www.fjorukrain.is. Byddðasafn Hafnarfjörður: Vesturgata 8. Tel: 565 5420. www.hafnarfjordur.is/museum. Sívertsen House open: Jun–Aug daily 1–5pm; May & Sept Sat–Sun 1–5pm; Oct–Apr by arrangement. Siggubær's Pakkhúsið open: Jun–Aug daily 11am–5pm; Sept–May Sat–Sun 11am–7pm.

Hafnarborg: Strandgata 34. Tel: 585 5790. www.hafnarborg.is. Open: Mon, Wed & Fri–Sun noon–5pm, Thur noon–9pm. Free admission. Bus from Reykjavík: S1.

Keflavík

People mostly know Keflavík because it is the site of the international airport but the town has several attractions beyond the regular landings and take-offs of planes. The largest town on the peninsula, it is known not only because of the airport but also due to its proximity to the large American-dominated NATO base, which shut down its operations in 2006.

Statues looking out to sea at Keflavík

Around the capital

Visitors try to capture geothermal activity

The town's port is home to the *Íslendingur*, an authentic re-creation of an original Viking ship, that sailed from Iceland to the east coast of the United States in the year 2000. It is now housed in the new Vikingaheimar (**Viking World Museum**), based on an exhibition produced by the Smithsonian. It gives a great overview of Viking culture.

The art and cultural centre at **Duus Hús** has one of the most unusual collections in Iceland. The miniature boats on display are examples drawn from the entire history of Iceland's fishing fleet and were brought together by a former trawler captain for whom these models were a passion.

There is a small folk museum in **Ytri-Njarðvík**, a reconstructed turf farmhouse in neighbouring Njarðvík, but it is not open regular hours so consult the tourist office if you would like to make a visit.

Vikingaheimar (Viking World Museum): 1 Viking braut. Tel: 422 2000. www.vikingaheimar.com. Open: daily 11am–6pm. Admission charge.

Duus Hús (Duus House): Duusgata 2–10. Tel: 421 3796. Open: daily 11am–6pm. Free admission.

Ytri-Njarðvík: Stekkjarkot. Tel: 421 3796. Open: by arrangement. Admission charge.

Kerið Crater Site

A small but perfectly formed crater sits beside the main road between Selfoss and Laugarvatn, making it one of the easiest to visit for those who don't wish to walk far. There is a viewing platform but it is best not to walk around the rim as the ground is loose and the sides rather steep. This can be a stop on a day tour to Geysir and Gullfoss.

Open access. Free admission.

Mosfellsbær

This small town just north of the capital, almost part of Reykjavík's greater agglomeration, has little to attract visitors except for the fact that it was home to one of Iceland's greatest 20th-century sons.

Pride of place in Mosfellsbær goes to **Gljúfrasteinn**, home of Nobel Prize winner and author Halldór Laxness (1902–98), and now open to the public as the **Laxness Museum**. The house was built in 1945 in the plain functional style of that time. Halldór spent his last years here and the rooms have been preserved as the author had them, including the study upstairs with his books and personal items. This room also has a collection of works of art by his peers, among them Jóhannes Kjarval (*see p48*). The museum includes a multimedia presentation about the life of the author set against the larger socio-economic context that defined his work. His vintage Jaguar is still parked outside.

Gljúfrasteinn: 270 Mosfellsbær. Tel: 586 8066. www.gljufrasteinn.is. Open: Jun–Aug daily 9am–5pm; Sept–May Tue–Sun 10am–5pm. Summer concerts Sun 4pm. Admission charge.

Skálholt Cathedral is an important attraction in the region

Reykjanes Geothermal Area

One of Iceland's most active geothermal areas, the Reykjanes Peninsula sits on the westernmost landward section of the continental rift. It is volcanically active – as witnessed by the numerous and widespread lava fields and geothermic fields that feed the Blue Lagoon (*see p58 & p75*) in addition to heating local homes.

Besides the steaming pools that feed the lagoon, there are two other areas of natural geothermal activity: **Gunnuhver**, west of Grindavík, and close to the southwest point of the peninsula; and **Seltún**, east of the same town. These are generally much less visited than the Geysir and Strokkur site so you can spend time here simply marvelling at nature's wonder.

THE BRIDGE BETWEEN TWO CONTINENTS

A narrow metal bridge spans the narrow divide between the North American and European plates and you can walk between the two without carrying a passport! Once you've crossed, head to the information office at Reykjanesbær (*Hafnargargötu 57, Keflavík*) to get a certificate of the event!
The bridge is situated south of Keflavík off route 425. Open access. Free admission.

Just north of the Seltún field is Krýsuvíkurkirkja, a diminutive black painted church dating from 1861; sadly, though, it is rarely open. *Open access to both areas. Free admission.*

Selfoss

The largest town in southern Iceland, Selfoss is the centre of Iceland's dairy industry but has little to hold a tourist's interest. Just a little way southwest of the city, on the Ölfusá River that the town flanks, is the **Flói Nature Reserve**, an important marshland environment for migratory bird populations.

Skálholt Cathedral

The southern seat of the Catholic bishops of Iceland – whose northern seat is at Hólar (*see pp95–6*) – this site was of paramount importance to Iceland's religious life in the years 1056–1550. The last Catholic bishop, Jón Arason, along with two of his sons, was beheaded here in 1550 on the orders of the Danish Crown, in a final act to put down the Catholic faith and herald the victory of the Lutheran Reformation.

The original cathedral on the site was taken down in the 18th century and today's church, though of course a Protestant place of worship, did not replace it until the 1950s. The site has a small museum related to the Reformation, a plaque to Jón, and the tomb of another bishop, Páll Jónsson (a

religious leader in the early 13th century), which was found during the extensive and still ongoing archaeological excavations.

The Icelandic Lutheran Church runs the surrounding complex as a camp and educational facility for children. *Tel: 486 8870. www.skalholt.is. Service every Sun plus morning and evening plays on weekdays. Summer concerts.*

Þingvellir *(see also p54)*

Þingvellir was the original site of the historic Icelandic Parliament, the Alþing, the first democratic governmental structure that the world had seen when it was founded in 930. It's a significant national park for Icelanders because of this cultural history as well as the breathtaking landscape, beloved of hikers, geologists and birdwatchers. The pastureland that was the meeting place of the Parliament sits in a wide valley by the banks of Lake Þingvallavatn and directly on the continental rift, where North America and Europe are gradually moving apart at the rate of a millimetre a year.

You can stand on the **Lögberg**, or 'Law Rock', where proclamations of the laws passed were made; the site is marked by a flagpole. There are also a few remains of numerous *búðir*, where the delegates would stay during the proceedings.

Modern Icelanders consider this site the symbolic heart of the country and gather here in thousands on important

The Oxara River in Þingvellir National Park

occasions such as the founding day
of independent Iceland in 1944, and
in 2000 to celebrate a millennium
of Christianity.

Declared a UNESCO World
Heritage Site in 2004, it includes an
old parsonage and a national graveyard
where several luminaries now rest.
The most traditional building is
Þingvellabær, a farmhouse built in
1930 to commemorate the first meeting
of the Alþing. The farmhouse recalls
the fact that in 930 these fields were
part of private farmland owned by a

settler. Þingvellabær is now used as a
summer residence by the prime
minister of Iceland.

The **National Park Information
Office** has information about the
history and the landscape of the region.
There are many easy and enjoyable
walks that are accessible to even the
most physically unfit.

To the northwest of the site of the
Alþing is the western wall of the
continental rift along the Almannagjá
(Everyman's) fault. The **Hakið
Interpretive Centre** screens a regular

video show explaining how the fault works. The most exciting part of this visit is to walk on the wall of the fissure itself – standing on North American land and looking eastward to Europe only a few hundred metres away across the continental divide.

South of the Alþing site is **Þingvallavatn**, over 80sq km (31sq miles) of fresh water sitting on the rift. In recent years it has become a key dive site, where you can descend to the depths of the **Silfra rift** and see water bubble up between the Eurasian and American tectonic plates. There are a couple of volcanic islands and a geothermal field on route 360, on the western flank. Close by is a small copse of trees surrounded by a wall and

marked by a phalanx of national flags. This is **Vinaskógur**, or 'friends' wood'. All the trees planted here are gifts to the incumbent president of Iceland from foreign dignitaries. The grove was started on the 60th birthday of President Vigdís Finnbogadóttir with a gift of several birch trees from an Irish ambassadorial delegation.

Þingvellir Visitor Centre: tel: 482 2660.
www.thingvellir.is. Open: May–Sept
daily 9am–4pm. Free admission.
Hakið Interpretive Centre:
open: Apr–Oct daily 9am–4pm.
Free admission.
Vinaskógur: open access.
Free admission.
Silfra rift: tel: 663 2858. www.dive.is.
Free admission.

Around the capital

The entrance to 'friends' wood' (Vinaskógur)

Pagan religion

Religion was an important aspect of the daily life of Vikings. A panoply of gods controlled their everyday lives, the seasons and the results of their raids and conquests. The pagan religion of the Vikings, though long dead, has left behind a legacy. Many of the days of the week in the English calendar are named after these northern gods, who used to be worshipped by the Norse and their Saxon cousins.

How the world was created

According to the religion of the Vikings, the universe was made up of many regions. To the south was a bright, warm land where the fire giant Muspel had his domain. In the north was a place of cold and darkness ruled by a goddess called Hel. This was the place where those who did not die the death of a warrior would spend eternity.

In this 18th-century Icelandic illustration, Thor is shown with his hammer Mjolnir, wearing his belt of strength

At the dawn of time there was nothing between these two realms but empty space. However, along came Ymir, who brought forth the Norse gods and giants. The chief god Odin killed Ymir and created Midgard or 'Middle Earth' – the realm that filled the void – from Ymir's remains.

After Odin created Middle Earth, he built Asgard, the home of the gods. There was a home for each of them plus a special place for the Viking warriors who died in battle. The place was called Valhalla. A special force of women warriors called Valkyries made decisions about who would be victorious in battle and who could be admitted into Valhalla.

Eventually, time would end when the giants of the cold land and the giants of the hot land would clash in cataclysmic battle. This was called Ragnarök, the end of the worlds – except that the cycle would then start all over again.

The gods

Odin Chief of the gods, Odin had gained wisdom and cunning by drinking from the sacred spring. The runes (see p17) were revealed to Odin

and they became magical symbols and a secret code. Odin's Saxon name was Woden, from which the English Wednesday is derived.

Thor Son of Odin, Thor was the strongest of the gods and is depicted holding a hammer. Thunder was his weapon and he was often entreated by humans during vicious storms. Thor was put through many trials by the evil 'world serpent' Jörmungandr, who tried to usurp his power. They met in a final tumultuous battle at Ragnarök. Thor is remembered in the English Thursday.

Freya Freya was the goddess of love and extremely beautiful. She is remembered in the English Friday.

Tyr Another son of Odin, Tyr was the god of war. His Saxon name was Tiu and he gave his name to the English Tuesday.

Sol and Mani Sol and Mani were the sun and the moon, set in the sky by Odin when he created Middle Earth. Both drove chariots in great haste across the sky because they were being chased by evil wolves. When Ragnarök arrived the wolves would catch them both, and day and night would cease to exist. In Saxon the sun and moon were called Sunne and Mona, giving us the English Sunday and Monday.

SO THAT'S WHY!

The Viking pagan midwinter celebration was known as Jul, and is carried on in our modern yuletide greetings around Christmas time.

Drives: The Golden Circle Route and the Reykjanes Peninsula

There are two excellent drives that will bring you face to face with the real Iceland – a country of volcanoes and fishing and, once you are outside of Reykjavík 101, a land of small-town living.

Distance: 440km (273 miles).

EXPLORING THE GOLDEN CIRCLE ROUTE AT LEISURE

It is much more pleasant to do this at your own pace rather than being marched in and out of expensive tour buses. Have a picnic at the Parliament fields. Meditate to the sounds of a geyser or magnificent waterfall.

Start out from Reykjavík after a hearty breakfast. Leave by Miklabraut, then Reykjanesbraut, following the signs to route 1 and Selfoss. Once on route 1, head southeast, initially following the same signs. After 17km (11 miles), you will pass signs for the Svínahraun Ski area to your left. After a further 16km (10 miles), you will reach Hveragerði.

1 Hveragerði

Hveragerði is a small town that makes a living from geothermally heated glass houses. It's a very active volcanic area and earthquakes regularly happen. Visit the tourist office (*Sunnumörk 2. Tel: 483 4000. www.hveragerdi.is*) to find out more about viewing the active hot springs.

Continue on route 1 for another 11km (7 miles) and just before reaching Selfoss turn left on route 35. Drive on and after 8km (5 miles) you will cross the River Sog. After about 4km (2½ miles), you will find the car park of the Kerið Crater Site on your right.

2 Kerið Crater Site

This small crater site is a suitable stop for volcano enthusiasts.
Continue north on route 35 for another 23km (14 miles) and then turn right on to route 31. Just a couple of kilometres after the junction, Skálholt comes into view on the right.

3 Skálholt

This Lutheran complex was built in the last few years but stands on the site of a Catholic bishopric. Visit the 20th-century church to find items from those earlier times, including the tomb of an 13th-century bishop.
Return to route 35 and turn right. The road becomes increasingly rural and

*asphalt turns to dirt on short sections.
Keep following the signs for Gullfoss (you
will pass the Geysir site on the left but we
will return here soon).*

4 Gullfoss

Gullfoss is an impressive sight but the
sound of the waters hits you well before
the falls come into view. The water fans
out over two small curtain falls before
dropping into a narrow chasm and
disappearing from view.

*Leave Gullfoss by the same road as you
came and this time stop at Geysir and
Strokkur.*

5 Geysir and Strokkur

Geysir is the most famous geyser in the
world but now it is a spent force.

Strokkur, however, performs at least
once every ten minutes, day or night.
Enjoy the surrounding geothermal
pools and flumes.

*Turn left out of the Geysir car park and
follow the signs to Laugarvatn on route 37.
Laugarvatn is 37km (23 miles) from
Gullfoss.*

6 Laugarvatn

Laugarvatn is a small summer resort
with a spa that is popular with people
from the capital.

*At Laugarvatn, turn right on route 365
in the direction of Þingvellir National
Park. This road leads you through some
wild landscapes. After 16km (10 miles),
you will reach the junction of route 36.
Take a right turn here. You will see the*

Drives: The Golden Circle Route and the Reykjanes Peninsula

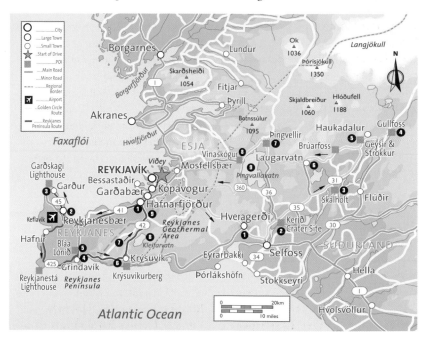

Visitor Centre and car park signposted on the left after 8km (5 miles).

7 Þingvellir

The buildings at þingvellir, the 'Parliament fields', are picture-perfect. Enjoy taking a stroll on the continental rift and the views across the lake.
Return from the car park to route 36. Turn left and follow the road. After 9km (5½ miles), you will see Vinaskógur on the right.

8 Vinaskógur

Vinaskógur, or 'friends' wood', is a copse of trees given as gifts to the president of Iceland by visiting dignitaries.
Just beyond Vinaskógur turn left on route 360.

9 Þingvallavatn

Route 360 skirts the shores of Lake Þingvallavatn in a roller-coaster ride past numerous small summer cabins owned by wealthy Icelanders from Reykjavík, and a small geothermal site. There are good lake views between the shrubs and copses.
After 10km (6 miles), there is a right turn to Reykjavík over the Mosfellsheiði.

A DRIVE AROUND REYKJANES PENINSULA

Begin by taking route 41 to nearby Hafnarfjörður, a harbour town where elves and fairies are said to lurk.
Leave Reykjavík taking route 41, signposted to Keflavík and the international airport. Even before the suburbs disappear behind you, you will see signs for Hafnarfjörður (about 5km/ 3 miles away on route 41). Take this road inland and head into the town.

1 Hafnarfjörður

Hafnarfjörður has a busy harbour and you will usually see some activity in the mornings with boats landing their catches. Visit the Hafnarfjörður Museum or Viking Village.
Return to route 41 and follow the signs for Keflavík. You will pass a municipal hoarding announcing that you are arriving in Reykjanesbær; after 25km (16 miles), you can turn right into the town.

2 Keflavík and Njarðvík

Keflavík and neighbouring Njarðvík seem to meet each other across the wide bay that used to separate them. Head to the harbour to see *Íslendingur*, the re-creation of an original Viking ship.
Return to route 41 and head west (left turn). You will pass the turning to the airport on the left; then take route 45 in the direction of Garður.

3 Garður Peninsula Historical Museum

Garður Peninsula Historical Museum and lighthouse make an interesting diversion, or you can head to the coast for some bird-spotting.
Retrace your drive past the airport and the Keflavík turning and, after 11km (7 miles), take a right turn at the junction for route 44; 4km (2½ miles) ahead, turn left on

route 425 in the direction of Grindavík. This route leads you through rugged coastal landscape before you reach the town.

4 Saltfish Museum

Visit the Saltfish Museum in Grindavík. *From Grindavík, it is only 6km (4 miles) or so along route 43 to the Blue Lagoon.*

5 Bláa Lónið (Blue Lagoon)

Stopping for a relaxing swim at the Blue Lagoon might sabotage your plans for the rest of the trip. You could spend an hour or two, or come back later for a fuller session. Eat at the on-site café or renowned Lava restaurant. *Return south to Grindavík and take route 427 east. Few tourists head this way even though it is so close to the capital. Turn left when you reach the junction of route 42. Just beyond the junction, you will see a small church on the left.*

6 Krýsuvíkurkirkja

This is Krýsuvíkurkirkja, one of the oldest wooden churches in Iceland and now a national monument. *Route 42 runs through the heart of the Reykjanesfólkvangur Natural Area. It is a seemingly desolate place but has some good walking routes. After another 3km (2 miles), the Reykjanes Geothermal Area comes into view.*

7 Reykjanes Geothermal Area

This is one of the more interesting geothermal regions visually because the plumes, pools and boiling pots rise up the hillside. *Continue on route 42 until you see Kleifarvatn on the right.*

8 Kleifarvatn

This starkly beautiful lake is set amid jet-black rocks. *Continue on route 42, which eventually leads you back to the southern suburbs of Hafnarfjörður. Just before you reach the urban sprawl, you will pass rows of wooden latticework on either side of the road.*

9 Fish-drying trestles

Drying fish in the open air is becoming less popular now but before the introduction of salting and freezing, it was the main method of preserving the product. *Route 42 will eventually meet route 41 where you can make a right turn, following signposts for the capital, Reykjavík.*

Krýsuvíkurkirkja is one of the oldest wooden churches in Iceland

Snæfellsnes and the Westfjords

Iceland's northwestern corner is a region shrouded in myths and of contrasting landscapes with solitary farmhouses, hidden valleys and indomitable cliffs. Snæfellsnes is easily reached from Reykjavík, whereas the Westfjords involves a serious journey – but the rewards for those who venture there are many!

The Snæfellsnes Peninsula points westward, north of Reykjavík, like a finger. It is a narrow yet varied world of cliffs, valleys and tiny towns set in the shadow of the brooding and mysterious Snæfellsjökull, a cone-shaped glacier.

The southern coastline of Snæfellsnes has some of Iceland's most dramatic lava fields stretching from the extinct crater to the sea. The rich blanket of mosses and lichens growing on the lunar landscape changes colour throughout the day, and the weird rock formations have given rise to tales of trolls and little people who are said to inhabit the numerous caves.

The northern coast of the peninsula is a total contrast, with rounded hills, sweeping lowland meadows and small towns forming the southern shore of the vast Breiðafjörður inlet and Hvammsfjörður, a region of scattered islands and islets. The mountain of **Kirkjufell** (463m/1,519ft) with its glorious curves is considered the most beautiful and is typical of the vista.

To the north of the Snæfellsnes, the Westfjords is the oldest part of Iceland. The land mass owes its glorious vistas to glaciation. Sheer cliffs that rise over 100m (328ft) directly from the ocean are tabletopped by thousands of hectares of upland moors carpeted with alpine tundra and often shrouded in mist. The Westfjords is sparsely populated with a handful of towns clinging limpet-like to the valley floors. The many abandoned farms stand witness to the recent depopulation and make the Westfjords seem all the more wild.

Linking the two regions is the low-lying meadowland of the Dalir, an area rich in *Saga* history, where Sturlungs – who controlled half of Iceland in the 13th century – had their power base.

Arnarstapi

This tiny collection of buildings set around a small rocky cove is one of the best places along the coast to stop for birdwatching. In the summer, the cliffs and offshore basalt stacks look like high-rise apartment blocks for seagoing birds as they circle in their thousands. On the cliff top stands a sturdy stone sculpture by Ragnar Kjartansson representing Bárður Snæfellsás, the guardian spirit of the region.

The 526m (1,726ft)-high **Stapafell** behind the cove is reputedly home to mischievous trolls. An unpaved road to the east of the hill leads up to the snowline at **Snæfellsjökull glacier**.

You can walk along the cliffs west of town for around 2.5km (1½ miles) to reach **Hellnar**, a small fishing town, passing some of the region's most dramatic volcanic landscapes where the power of the ocean has eroded the lava flows into surreal columns and razor-edged ridges. Hellnar was the home of Guðriður Þorbjarnardóttir, who, according to accounts, was the first European woman to give birth on North American soil when she travelled to Vinland in 1004. A small plaque close to the main road marks the location of the family farm.

Bolungarvík

One of Iceland's oldest fishing communities, Bolungarvík hugs the water's edge in the shadow of Traðarhyna Hill to the northwest of Ísafjörður.

(*Cont. on p80*)

For the drive route, see pp78–9

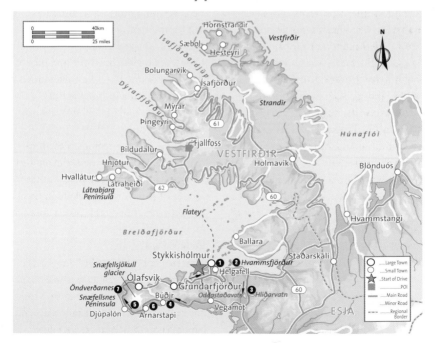

Drive: Snæfellsnes Peninsula

The Snæfellsnes Peninsula makes for an excellent day tour, as most of the major attractions lie just a stone's throw away from the main route. It is also possible to do this tour in a day from Reykjavík – though you would need to get an early start. (The route is shown on the map on p77.)

Time: 8 hours.

Distance: 270km (168 miles).

Start the journey at Stykkishólmur.

1 Helgafell
Leave the town heading south, past the sacred mound of Helgafell, until you reach the intersection of route 54 where you will turn left. You can stop off at Stykkishólmur for coffee or a birdwatching boat trip, too.

2 Hvammsfjörður
As you travel along the route, you will find outstanding views across Hvammsfjörður with its myriad tiny islands. Look out for seals basking on the rocky shoreline.
Drive along the coast road with the waters on your left until you reach the junction of route 55 heading south to Borgarnes. Turn right here and the road climbs up the Heydalur into barren hinterland.

3 Oddastaðavatn and Hlíðarvatn
At the highest point on the cross-peninsula road lie the twin lakes of Oddastaðavatn and Hlíðarvatn, surrounded by an almost lunar landscape and dramatic ancient volcanoes. After the lakes, the route drops through the vast lava fields of Koleinsstaðahreppur, to meet route 54 again.
Turn right. After 25km (16 miles), you will pass a right turn for Stykkishólmur. Ignore this and continue on. The road weaves across the coastal plain passing several lakes and offering tantalising glimpses of Snæfellsjökull up ahead. After a further 37km (23 miles), route 54 turns inland to Ólafsvík and Hellissandur. Bear left on route 574 signposted Arnarstapi. Watch out for another turning left to Buðir just a little further along.

4 Buðir church
Buðir church is reached by traversing the Buðahraun lava flow. Park here and walk the short way beyond the church and across the reddish sand dunes blanketed in tussock grasses to the beach, the finest on the peninsula. People even swim here in summer.

Return to route 574 and turn left. Snæfellsjökull now looms ahead and you will see the route up to the mountain on your right after 12km (7 miles). This road is unpaved and closed in winter.

5 Snæfellsjökull glacier

You can get close-up views of the snow cap and a chance to walk on the pumice slopes – rocks that were ejected when the volcano last blew its top.

Return to route 574, less than 1km (½ mile) ahead, and take the left turn to Arnarstapi.

6 Arnarstapi

Arnarstapi is a diminutive rocky port set amid amazing basalt rock formations – volcanic lava pounded by waves for millennia have created caves and stacks in abundance. You can almost touch the nesting seabirds here. The coastal walk west to Hellnar is worth it if you have the time (a couple of hours' return trip).

The main road sweeps on in the shadow of the great crater. At the northwestern corner of the peninsula, the road doglegs inland across a flat plain punctuated by smaller pseudo-craters. As you reach the coast, take the left turn.

7 Öndverðarnes

The cliffs around Öndverðarnes point are known as 'the black skies' in Icelandic, because they are so dark and foreboding. There have been many shipwrecks off this dramatically beguiling spot.

After Öndverðarnes, the road turns abruptly east to follow the northern coast. You will pass the towns of Hellissandur and Ólafsvík with their small museums before you leave Snæfellsjökull behind and verdant glacial valleys lead you back to Stykkishólmur.

Buðir church

Fjallfoss waterfall

The town's **Náttúrugripasafn Bolungarvíkur** (Natural History Museum) offers a collection of stuffed birds and animals including an unfortunate polar bear shot as it made a diversion from the snowfields of Greenland.

The more interesting **Ósvör** (outside Bolungarvík) brings the salt-fishing industry to life. Housed in an old fisherman's hut, the museum includes everyday artefacts and a salt-fishing shed that smells like the real thing! The colourful curator is full of historical lore. The town was the location for Dagur Kári's film *Nói Albinói*.

There is a monument to businessman Einar Guðfinsson (1898–1985) on the waterfront. *Náttúrugripasafn Bolungarvíkur: Vitastigúr 3. Tel: 456 7507. www.natturgripasafn.is. Open: mid-Jun–mid-Aug daily 9am–5pm; mid-Aug–mid-Jun by arrangement. Ósvör: tel: 892 5744. http://osvor.is. Open: early Jun–mid-Aug daily 10am–5pm; mid-Aug–early Jun by arrangement. Admission charge.*

Búðir

A tiny anchorage on the southern coast of the Snæfellsnes, Búðir sits in the heart of a protected area of a volcanic lava field. There is nothing left of the village now save a tiny 19th-century church, one of the few in Iceland that were built by a private individual without the authority of the Icelandic Lutheran Church. Walk past the church to the black-sand beach, which stretches east around the peninsula. You can stop for lunch or coffee and cake at the stylish Hotel Búðir, a renowned hotel for weekending Reykjavíkers, just before the church.

Fjallfoss

The Westfjords' largest waterfall is easy to find. The main road runs right by and there is ample parking at the base. The 100m (328ft)-high and very broad falls that break into several separate white cascades are also known as Dynjandi, meaning 'resounding', for their sound that can be heard throughout the surrounding valleys.

Flatey

The only populated island in Breiðafjörður, Flatey was home to some of Iceland's first settlers when a community of Irish monks established a monastery here in 1172. They did not stay long, moving to Helgafell as early as 1184. The town became an official trading post in 1777 and was a cultural centre during the 19th century, housing Iceland's first library, but it is a sleepy backwater today. There are many period houses to enjoy in the town and the parish church features a fresco by contemporary artist Baltasar. You can also head out on foot to enjoy easy walks.

You can reach Flatey from Stykkishólmur (*see pp86–7*) on the northern Snæfellsnes Peninsula or Brjánslækur on the southern coast of the Westfjords on the daily ferry *Baldur* (*Tel: 433 2254. www.saeferdir.is. Departures Jun–Aug 9am & 4pm*).

To the west of Flatey are the waters of Breiðafjörður scattered with small islands that are home to large populations of seabirds.

Holmavík

This one-horse town on the southeastern coast of the Westfjords could be easily bypassed were it not for a fascinating little exhibition. The **Galdrasýning á Ströndum** (Museum of Icelandic Sorcery and Witchcraft) is the result of one man's obsession with the tradition of witchcraft in Iceland. The museum explains the traditions of sorcery – which, unusually, was controlled by men here in contrast to witchcraft in other countries, which tended to be the women's domain – and charts the witchcraft accusations and trials that swept Iceland, and particularly the Strandir region (*see pp141–3*), during the 17th century. In a frenzy that matched the zeal of the Inquisition, over 20 people were burnt at the stake and many more flogged. More often than not, the accusations related to Norse pagan practices

and rituals carried on through the ages, but some seemed to have a 'supernatural' basis.

The museum has some unusual artefacts including an ancient 'blood stone' where sacrifices (of animals) were made; there are also modern re-creations of certain so-called magical practices that took place in these parts. The exhibition is best experienced with the English commentary (*extra charge*), which does an excellent job of explaining the background to the events, and the role that magic and superstition played in the lives of Icelanders at that time.

The museum has a second exhibit, the Sorcerer's Cottage, located at Bjarnarfjörður, 30km (19 miles) north into the Strandir, and there are plans to open others around the region. *Galdrasýning á Ströndum: Höfðagata 8–10. Tel: 451 3525. www.galdrasyning.is. Open: Jun–mid-Sept daily 10am–6pm; mid-Sept–Jun by arrangement. Admission charge.*

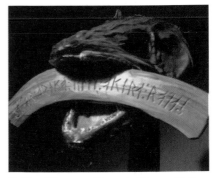

Traditional items used to control the weather, from the Witchcraft Museum

Snæfellsnes and the Westfjords

The historic houses of Ísafjörður

Hvammsfjörður

Hvammsfjörður forms a narrow inlet at the southeastern head of Breiðafjörður on the Snæfellsnes Peninsula. This was one of the centres of action during the old *Saga* (*see pp28–9*) days. Snorri Sturluson (*see p29*) was born in the countryside at the head of the fjord, and the rolling farmland was the setting for the *Laxædala Saga* telling tales of several generations of Icelandic farmers.

Hvammsfjörður has hundreds of islets, though some of them are mere sentinel rocks, that play host to some of the richest bird populations in Iceland. These can be seen from the mainland, most easily from the northern coast of the Snæfellsnes Peninsula east of Stykkishólmur.

Ísafjörður

This pleasant little town occupying one of the most dramatic settings anywhere

in Iceland is the capital of the Westfjords. Set on a natural coastal spit in Skutulsfjörður and surrounded by vertiginous glacial walls, it can only be reached from the south via a single-lane road tunnel cut through the heart of the Breiðadalsheiðdi uplands that hem it in to the south. Inland from the spit is the Westfjords, one of the most sheltered natural harbours, and the approach to the tiny airfield across the town and close to the valley sides is one of the most exciting anywhere!

Hanseatic League traders used to live here in the 16th century, but they set up camp only in summer. The town was one of six that was given a licence following the abolition of the trade monopoly in 1786, and it developed thereafter.

Hæstikaupstaður at Aðalstræti 42 was built by the first commercial merchants in 1788 but Ísafjörður always made a living from the sea and things haven't really changed even today. Whaling was a major industry and the town was at the centre of the decision to restart 'scientific whaling' after more than a decade. Whaling still goes on today in the town.

The history of fishing is explored at the **Neðstikaupstaður** (Westfjords Heritage Museum), a complex of listed buildings and assorted fishing paraphernalia including several characterful wooden fishing boats. The main display is in Turnhús, an 18th-century warehouse.

The town has numerous pretty houses that date from the late 19th and early 20th centuries. Take the walk (*see* *pp88–9*) for some of the more picturesque examples.

There is a well-established ski station on the slopes above the town. Ísafjörður Ski Week, held over Easter, is the highlight of the winter season when competitions on the piste and arts exhibitions, musical performances and a party atmosphere invade the town.

Situated 4km (2½ miles) north of the town, the village of **Hnífsdalur** is a centre of production for *hákarl* shark (putrefied). Admittedly, it is an acquired taste but you will find it nowhere else but in Iceland.

In addition to the route from the south, Ísafjörður is linked to the outside world by route 61 leading east in and

A trawler in Ísafjörður

Ólafsvík scenery

out of the sub-fjords that sprout from Ísafjörðardjúp, a wide exit to the Atlantic. It is a majestic landscape of wide glacial valleys punctuated by small farmsteads. At the outlet of Skötufjörður above the road is the turf farmhouse of **Litlbær**. Now owned by the National Museum of Iceland, this small collection of buildings from the late 1800s was home to two families until 1969.
Neðstikaupstaður: Suðurgata. Tel: 456 3293. www.nedsti.is. Open: Jun–Aug Mon–Fri 10am–5pm, Sat–Sun 1–5pm. Admission charge.

Tourist office: Aðalstræti 7. Tel: 450 8060. www.iatfjordir.is

Ólafsvík

Issued a trade licence in 1687, the old warehouse of **Gamla Pakkhúsið** harks back to an era of wealth; it was built in 1841 by the Clausen family, then the leading commercial entrepreneurs of the town. The building now houses the tourist office and the Snæfellsbæjar Regional Museum, with folklore galleries and artefacts of local life and lifestyle.
Gamla Pakkhúsið (Old Warehouse): Ólafsbraut. Tel: 436 1650.
Open: Jun–Aug daily 9am–7pm. Admission charge.

Snæfellsjökull National Park

The archetypal volcanic cone of Snæfellsjökull (1,446m/4,744ft), which can easily be seen from Reykjavík acts as a magnet attracting travellers north. The barely dormant volcano is shrouded in myth. It was a totem to the Norsemen, who thought it to be the home of trolls; is considered a powerful source of positive energy by 'new-

COLUMBUS DOES HIS HOMEWORK

It is believed that Christopher Columbus visited a previous church on the site of Ingjaldhóll in 1477 when he came to consult the *Sagas* about routes to west Vinland in preparation for his own epic voyage of discovery. A painting in the church depicts his meeting with the local clergymen but there is no record of whether he learnt anything that proved to be of value to him when he sailed.

agers'; and was the setting for Jules Verne's *Journey to the Centre of the Earth*, where the explorers set out to the earth's belly by climbing down the volcano's 1km (½-mile) -wide crater.

That the volcano was active till very recently (in geological time at least) is evidenced by the layers of petrified lava flowing from every face. The western faces look like the surface of the human brain with rivulets of molten rock that have hardened and rounded as they dried. Atop this is a gleaming white snow cap, one of Iceland's smallest but prettiest glaciers.

To the northwest of the peak itself, the lava flows stretch out across a *sandur* to the high black basalt cliffs at

Öndverðarnes where a couple of lighthouses protect shipping from the treacherous waters. There are several walking routes around the pseudo-craters here or along the coast past the highest structure on the island, a 420m (1,378ft) long-wave radio mast, to Hellissandur with **Sjomannagarður**, its small turf-roofed maritime museum (*Hellissandur, on the main coast road. Tel: 436 6860. Open: Jun–Aug Tue–Sun 9am–6pm. Admission charge*).

From Arnarstapi, various tour operators run Ski-doo tours of the glacier, too. The church at Ingjaldhóll just beyond the town is said to be the oldest concrete church in Iceland, erected in 1903.

Snæfellsjökull glacier, which can be seen from Reykjavík, atop the dormant volcano

Strandir (*see pp53, 81 & 141–3*)

Stykkishólmur

A municipality only since 1987, Stykkishólmur is nonetheless the leading town on the Snæfellsnes Peninsula. It is set on a short peninsula jutting into Breiðafjörður on the north of the Snæfellsnes so has panoramic sea views to the north and west.

Boats moored in the harbour at Stykkishólmur

The oldest building in the town, **Norska Húsið** (Norwegian House), was imported from Bergen in 1832 by Árni Thorlacius, considered the 'father of Stykkishólmur'. It houses a collection of furniture and artefacts donated by or rescued from local households. Árni used to take daily meteorological readings during his youth, a practice that continues to this day; these form an invaluable resource to meteorological scientists.

Vatnasafn (Library of Water), Stykkishólmur's most modern cultural attraction, is a permanent sculpture installation and community centre and is located in the town's former library building, overlooking the ocean and harbour.

The American artist Roni Horn, in collaboration with London-based arts group Artangel, developed a constellation of glass columns containing glacial water from around Iceland. Through these columns, natural light is refracted and reflected on to the specially created floor inscribed with both Icelandic and English words to describe the weather or the mood of the viewer. The visitor is absorbed into a world of weather, water and light in a refuge of solitary reflection.

The ferry *Baldur* links Stykkishólmur with the Westfjords in a three-hour trip, with a port of call at Flatey Island (*see pp80–81*).

Inland from the town is a small hill called **Helgafell** that was sacred to the people of the *Saga* era. It was the home of Snorri goði (the northern tribal chief in the *Eyrbyggja Saga*) and the final resting place of Guðrún Ósvifursdóttir (of the *Laxdæla Saga*).

Fifteen kilometres (nine miles) west of Stykkishólmur lies the Berserkjahraun or Berserks lava field, scene of a famous incident in *Eyrbyggja Saga*. The farmer of Hraun returned from Norway with a couple of men. But they took a shine to his daughter. The farmer set them what he thought was an impossible task – to clear a path through the lava fields to his brother's farm – and offered his daughter's hand in marriage to the man who could do the job. The task was completed in record time, but the farmer reneged on his deal and his daughter married Snorri goði instead! *Norska Húsið: Hafnargata 5. Tel: 438 1640. Open: May–Sept daily 11am–5pm; Oct–Apr by arrangement. Admission charge. Vatnasafn: Bókhloðustigur 17. www.libraryofwater.is. Open: Jun–Aug daily 1–6pm; May & Sept Sat–Sun 1–6pm; Oct–Apr Sat 2–6pm.*

GETTING AROUND

If you would rather let someone else take the driving strain, try the Snæfellsjökull bus that does a complete lap of the western Snæfellsnes. You can buy a circuit ticket that allows you to get off one day and continue the journey the next; so you can enjoy a morning walk at Arnarstapi, for instance.
The bus runs from Reykjavík's central bus station. *Tel: 551 1166. www.sterna.is*

Snæfellsnes and the Westfjords

Walk: Ísafjörður

A trading port since the mid-16th century, Ísafjörður has a dramatic setting on a natural spit surrounded by the sheer walls of a glacial valley. It has been a seafaring town through the 20th century and is the administrative capital of the Westfjords. The compact town retains some interesting domestic architecture, much of which is still used as family homes.

Time: 1½ hours. Distance: 1.5km (1 mile).

Start at the Whalebone arch at the main roundabout as you enter the town centre.

1 Whalebone arch

This arch is a testament to Ísafjörður's role as a Norwegian whaling station in the latter part of the 20th century. The town has courted some controversy since 2003 when the government voted to restart a small whaling programme. *Look north from the arch and across the street: at the corner of the open green parkland is a bronze statue. Cross the street to reach it.*

2 Hafnarstræti Monument

This depiction of sturdy seamen pays tribute to the Ísafjörðurs who set sail into harsh waters. Many never returned. *Walk left from the monument along Hafnarstræti. Across the park to your right stands the library.*

3 Hafnarstræti Library

This is a fine neoclassical structure, housing a folklore museum.

Carry on along Hafnarstræti and turn right at the next intersection along Túngata.

4 Túngata

The mansions of Túngata form one of the most architecturally complete streets in Iceland. Though not the oldest in town, they are copies of the catalogue houses brought by traders from Scandinavia.
Walk along Túngata. Turn right along Eyrargata, then right again at Kirkjugata. Turn left and walk past the church to the roundabout, then cross Sólgata to reach the oldest part of Ísafjörður. Take the first left, Hrannargata, then turn right along Fjarðarstræti and right again into Managata.

5 Managata

Most of the houses here date back to the 17th and 19th centuries. They range from humble cottages to larger buildings like the Gamla Guest House at Managata 5 (*www.gistihus.is*), which was originally built to accommodate Scandinavian traders.

Turn left where Managata meets Hafnarstræti and stay on this route. Turn left at Austurvegur, then right at Tangagata and right to Silfurgata.

6 Silfurgata

Silfurgata has another ensemble of period properties. The depth and completeness of this district makes it one of few such left in Iceland.

The end of Silfurgata links with Hafnarstræti. Turn left here and continue past the post office.

Hafnarstræti then becomes Aðalstræti, and where this road meets the coast road Póligata you will find the Tourist Office.

7 Tourist Office

The Tourist Office is housed in probably the finest single building in Ísafjörður, a clapboard mansion and trading post built in 1781.

From the Tourist Office, walk straight ahead into the warehouse area. The street is called Suðurgata but there are no signs. After 300m (984ft) or so, the Westfjords Maritime Museum will come into view.

8 Westfjords Maritime Museum

This is one of the prime museums outside Reykjavík, important principally for its collection of historic buildings, the youngest of which dates from 1784.

Walk: Ísafjörður

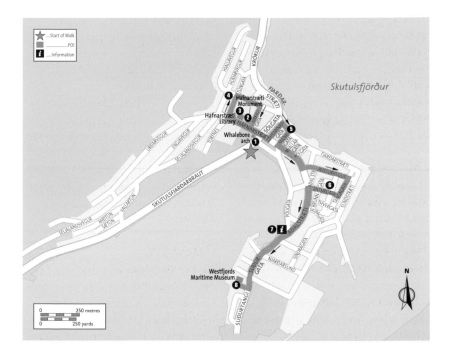

Northern Iceland

The attractions of Iceland's northern region are manifold. The major towns nestle on the banks of its rolling fjords while traditional farms sit square in the verdant meadowlands just in from the coast. Volcanic activity has given rise to some amazing natural features, while Captain Ahab would have been speechless at the sea mammal numbers offshore.

Akureyri

Iceland's second city, Akureyri, is a worthy runner-up to Reykjavík and is the undisputed cultural capital of the north. The town sits at the head of Eyjafjörður and has a reputation for a mean pub crawl (*see p153*).

The town's arts scene is second only to Reykjavík's with a professional theatre company and a summer festival that runs throughout the summer. Exhibitions are centred in **Listafnið** (Art Gallery) and **Listagil** (Arts Centre) in the heart of town. Next to the Edda Hotel is a sculpture park with works by most of Iceland's major talents.

The oldest part of the town is a 15-minute walk from the south of the town centre. The Main Street here (Aðalstræti) was the heart of the town a century ago and a series of clapboard houses still stand as testament. **Nonnahús** (Nonni's House) was the childhood home of Jón Sveinsson. The tiny wooden house, built around 1850, is a typical dwelling of its type. It has manuscripts of Nonni's many children's books and some of the author's personal artefacts. Outside the dwelling is his life-size statue.

Behind Nonni's House is **Akureyri Museum**, a rather nondescript building that houses a very good exhibition relating to the development of the

NONNI

Nonni was born in 1857 and moved to the house in Akureyri when he was eight years old, but after his father died in 1868 his mother was unable to cope with the household. A French nobleman offered to pay for the boy's education and Nonni went abroad in 1870. After finishing school he became a Jesuit priest and went on to higher levels of study in France, Denmark and England, and teaching in Catholic schools; he spent almost 20 years in Denmark.

In 1912, he gave up teaching and began writing and lecturing. He wrote 12 books that have been translated into 30 languages, and delivered over 5,000 lectures. Nonni returned to Iceland in 1930 to celebrate the 1,000-year anniversary of the Icelandic Alþing. He died in Cologne in 1944.

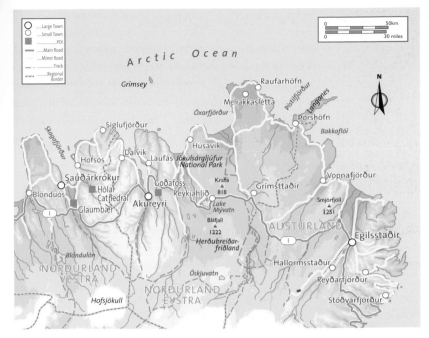

town, with artefacts from the early
settlement days to the 20th century.
Iðnaðarsafnið (the Industrial
Museum) concentrates on the area's
recent industrial successes. The regional
airport also has a collection relating to
20th-century technological successes.
Flugsafn Íslands (the Aviation Museum)
charts the development of commercial
flight in the country.

Around the bay on the road to
Laufás (*see p99*) and Húsavík (*see
pp96–7*) is **Safnasafnið Museum** (the
Icelandic Folk Art Museum), one
of the most innovative and proactive
galleries in Iceland. Set in a large
mansion, the exhibitions of works by
artists and sculptors change every year
but always include a rotating exhibition

from the Icelandic Doll Museum.
*Nonnahús: Aðalstræti 54. Tel: 462 3555.
www.nonni.is. Open: Jun–Aug daily
10am–5pm; Sept–May by arrangement.
Admission charge.
Akureyri Museum: Aðalstræti 58.
Tel: 462 4162. www.akmus.is. Open:
Jun–mid-Sept daily 10am–5pm;
Oct–May Sat 2–4pm; rest of the year by
arrangement. Admission charge.
Iðnaðarsafnið: Krókeyri. Tel: 462 3600.
Open: Jun–mid-Sept daily 10am–5pm;
mid-Sept–May Sat 2–4pm.
Admission charge.
Flugsafn Íslands: Akureyrarflugvöllur.
Tel: 461 4400. www.flugsafn.is. Open:
Jun–Aug daily 11am–5pm; Sept–May
Sat 2–5pm or by arrangement.
Admission charge.*

Safnasafnið Museum: Svalbarðsströnd. Tel: 461 4066. www.safnasafnid.is. Open: May–end Sept daily 2–5pm. Closed during winter. Admission charge.

Dalvík

Much of Dalvík was destroyed in a devastating earthquake in 1934 so the town is not architecturally rich. But it certainly makes the most of its few claims to fame, the most impressive of which is that it was the birthplace of Jóhann Pétersson, also known as 'Jóhann the Giant', who was the second-tallest man in the world during his lifetime, reaching 2.34m (7ft 8in) in

Glaumbær farm

his youth. He made a living in the circus away from his homeland but returned in 1982 to spend the last two years of his life here. Visit the town's **Byggðasafnið Hvoll á Dalvík** (Hvoll Folk Museum) to find more details of the man's life, including photographs and clothing. The other prominent display in this museum is the painting of a polar bear that has nothing to do with Iceland; however, the seal displayed with it was caught in fishing nets close by despite having been scientifically tagged just a month earlier almost a thousand miles away – that's pretty impressive speed! In summer months you can take whale-watching trips from the town.

Byggðasafnið Hvoll á Dalvík: Hvoll v/Karlsrauðatorgi. Tel: 466 1497. www.dalvik.is/byggdasafn. Open: Jun–Aug daily 11am–6pm; Sept–May Sat 2–5pm. Admission charge.

Glaumbær farm (also known as Skagafjörður Folk Museum)

This collection of 18th- and 19th-century farm buildings is one of the largest and best-preserved in Iceland's Skagafjörður region, with an unusually long central corridor leading to nine rooms and a further four barns within the floor plan. Rooms 6 to 8 at the end of the corridor were the *baðstofa*, or farmstead, where the family ate and slept. It is said that these tiny rooms housed 22 people at one time. Each individual had his or her own cot-bed where a few personal belongings were

The Icelandic turf-roofed house

also kept, including an *askur*, or wooden bowl, in which meals were eaten. Glaumbær was a large farm with two guest rooms, one of which is the oldest section of the house dating to

THE TURF-ROOFED FARM

After the loss of much of their forests soon after settlement, Icelanders had to think carefully about what materials they could build their houses and farms with. The turf-style house, almost universal until the end of the 19th century, was made up of a thin layer of wood – often imported or even driftwood found along the coast – insulated and roofed by thick turf blocks that were held together by a living layer of grass. The roof slope was critical for the rainwater to drain away rather than soak into the soil. The farm was an interconnected maze of tiny rooms, often added to over time as the family expanded or when times were good.

1841, and a large pantry and kitchen. For most farmers, this was an unheard-of luxury.

Apart from the sheer scale of the building, Glaumbær is wonderfully decorated with the little knick-knacks, tools and valuables that a farmer's family would own. It is a very evocative collection and shows the creative capability of men for carving and women for needlepoint and lace-making among even the most humble Icelanders.

At the Glaumbær site, the **Áshús**, a clapboard house built in 1886, is open for sandwiches and snacks.

Glaumbær. Tel: 453 6173.
Open: Jun–mid-Sept daily 9am–6pm;
mid-Sept–May by arrangement.
Admission charge.

The Icelandic Emigration Centre at Hofsós

Goðafoss

One of the most accessible major falls in Iceland, Goðafoss is only metres from the ring road. It is a cascade of brown frothy water heading seaward from the **Ódáðahraun** hills. The falls are the so-called 'Waterfall of the Gods' because after the Lögsögumaður Þorgeir went to a meeting to declare Iceland a monotheist Christian country, he threw his pagan statues into these waters on his return journey home.

Grímsey

The country's only territory within the Arctic Circle, Grímsey is 40km (25 miles) north of mainland Iceland. Most visitors venture here for birdwatching – there are vast colonies of puffins, razorbills, guillemots and terns among others. The easiest way to reach Grímsey is by ferry from Akureyri or to fly there.

Hofsós

One of Iceland's oldest trading ports, a cluster of 18th-century original and replica buildings sit on either side of the narrow coastal inlet overlooking the harbour at Hofsós. The setting, minus the clutter of modern intrusions, shows pretty much what one of these many trading centres would have looked like in its heyday.

On the south side is **Frændgarður**, an 18th-century warehouse that is architecturally valuable and owned by the National Museum of Iceland. Next door to this is a replica of the **Nýja Konungsverslunarhúsið** (the King's Retail Store) that stood here throughout the 19th century.

Head north (you will need to head inland and cross the modern bridge) to find a collection of trader buildings that host **Vesturfarasetrið** (the

Icelandic Emigration Centre). The centre works in cooperation with the Skagafjörður Folk Museum and the latest exhibition, 'Prairies Wide and Free', is in the newly built King's Retail Store, a near-replica of a previous store as seen on early 19th-century photographs of the village centre. This exhibition tells the story of Icelandic settlers in North Dakota. Pictures, text and dramatic settings bring to life the stories of the Icelandic settlers and the changed way of life in their new home. The red, white and blue **Gamla Kaupfélagið** (the Old Co-op) dating from 1909 concentrates on the lives of the Icelandic settlers who moved to make a fresh start in the 'New World'. The photographs might be the most interesting to non-Icelandic speakers.

The centre also plays an integral part in genealogical research relating to the bloodline of Icelandic Americans and in forging links between the generations living on the island and in the USA.

Just south of the town is a tiny turf **Gröf chapel**, thought to be the oldest in Iceland.

Vesturfarasetrið: tel: 453 7935. www.hofsos.is. Open: Jun–end Aug daily 11am–6pm; Sept–May by arrangement. Museum: admission charge; genealogy room: free admission.

Hólar Cathedral

One of two Icelandic bishoprics during the Catholic era, the present **Lutheran Cathedral** was finished in 1763 during the bishopric of Gisli Magnússon in a late-Baroque style. The interior is rather plain but the earlier altarpiece (*c.* 1500) is wonderfully detailed with panels depicting scenes from the Bible.

The late-Baroque-style Hólar Cathedral

Several artefacts belong to Bishop Guðbrandur Þorláksson (bishop 1571–1627), a forward-thinking man for his time, who was the first person to create a map of Iceland. His *Guðbrandsbiblia* was the first Bible to be produced in the Icelandic language, in 1584. The portrait of the bishop is the oldest known portrait of an Icelander, painted in 1620.

Hólar Cathedral open: daily 9am–6pm. Guided tours are offered. Free admission.

Húsavík

'European Capital of Whale-Watching' is the town's self-appointed epithet and it is probably not far from the truth. The boats here can offer an over 96 per cent success rate because the town sits just below the busy seasonal migratory lanes that run through the nutrient-rich waters of the Arctic Circle, just north of town.

Húsavík used to be a major harvester of the sea but today the poacher has turned gamekeeper, and whale-watching craft of various descriptions set sail morning and afternoon in season, weather permitting.

Hvalasafnið á Húsavík (the Húsavík Whale Museum) is an award-winning non-profit exhibition that speaks of all

Húsavík harbour

Húsavík Whale Museum

things whale-connected, from their gargantuan size (shown through skeletons) to their habits and intelligence, with interactive and technological displays and dioramas. Some of the most touching footage is of whale hunting and mass whale strandings, which have still to be fully explained. You can also go whale-watching on dry land in their simulator room.

The town's **Byggðasafn Sudur** (Folk Museum) has several sections including a good maritime display, a collection of over 35,000 photographs and the district archives. The Natural History section has a stuffed polar bear. This unfortunate animal met its end at Grímsey (*see p94*) in 1969 after drifting south from Greenland.

Another rather off-the-wall collection in the town is **Hið Íslenzka Reðasafn** (Icelandic Phallological Museum), where the pagan power of phallology is celebrated with a range of

interesting representations. Look out also for the town church, which is a wonderful confection of gingerbread decoration built in 1907.

Hvalasafnið á Húsavík: Hafnarstétt 1.
Tel: 414 2800. www.whalemuseum.is.
Open: Jun–Aug daily 9am–7pm; May &
Sept 10am–5pm. Admission charge.
Byggðasafn Sudur: Stóragarði 17.
Tel: 464 1860. www.husmus.is.
Open: Jun–Aug daily 10am–6pm;
Sept–May Mon–Fri 9am–4pm.
Admission charge.
Hið Íslenzka Reðasafn: Héðinsbraut 3a.
Tel: 566 8668. www.phallus.is.
Open: 20 May–10 Sept daily noon–6pm.
Admission charge.

Jökulsárgljúfur National Park

Jökulsárgljúfur is at the same time one of the most visited places in Iceland and one of the least explored (*see also p141*). Protecting the ruggedly beautiful gorge of the **Jökulsá á Fjöllum** River, the valley bottom remains a world apart; but its major cascade, **Dettifoss** – a thundering force of sedimentary dun-brown water from the central glaciers that drops 44m (144ft) over a curtain of grey basalt – is a magnet for independent travellers and tour groups.

To the north, the head of the gorge has shifted in geologically recent times, leaving a dry false gorge, **Ásbyrgi**, where you can explore the flora and fauna that have colonised the valley floor in a series of marked footpaths.

Krafla volcano still has seismic activity in the area

Krafla

One of Iceland's most famous active volcanoes, Krafla is now also a centre of geothermal energy, harvesting the heat that nature offers. At the bottom of the hill is an active area of hotpot activity with boiling mud pools and smelly steam spouts. Head higher towards the **Krafla crater** and you will pass a geothermal power station started in 1974 but never completed because of seismic activity in the area. Carry on to reach the site of the mountain itself at 818m (2,684ft). There is a scientific station here that takes readings round the clock, so in principle if the road is open it is safe to visit. Just below the peak is the **Viti crater**, a sheer-sided hole with a pool of caustic liquid in its depths. There is a footpath up and around the crater's edge. A little further away from Krafla, a 15-minute walk from the car park, is the **Leirhnjúkur crater** past numerous hot vents. The bubbling mud tells you there is heat very close to the surface here, so stay on the well-trodden paths.

Lake Mývatn

Set at the heart of a volcanic and geothermal area and on the mid-Atlantic ridge surrounded by extensive lava fields, Lake Mývatn is one of the most unusual ecosystems in Iceland –

a shallow nutrient-rich lake that is one of the most important bird-breeding regions in the northern hemisphere.

Every year thousands of birds settle here, feeding on the algae that thrives in the warm water. Others compete with the char and trout for the millions of black flies whose presence often spoils the trip for humans – Mývatn means 'the lake of midges', so you know what to expect. The northwestern flank of the lake was designated a protected breeding area in 1974 and some areas are off-limits when the birds are nesting.

The most prominent of these is **Hverfjall crater**. Over 400m (1,312ft) high and 1km (⅔ mile) in diameter, it dominates the foreshore and is one of the best examples of a tephra crater in the world. The black ridges can be walked but stay on the trodden paths.

Just south of Hverfjall is the **Dimmuborgir** lava field where the molten lava has cooled and solidified into tall pillars and surreal shapes including one named Kirkjan because it resembles a church.

Closer to the shoreline on the lake's southern edge is a small park of pseudo-craters, **Skutustaðir**, set around a tiny body of water, **Stakhólstjörn**. The footpath here is a great place from where to appreciate Mývatn's unique ecosystem and environment.

Mývatn's only village is tiny **Reykjahlíð**. Take time to seek out the parish church that is surrounded by lava spewed in the dramatic eruption of the 1720s – the largest amount of lava ever emitted from one eruption as far as scientists can tell. The church is said to have been saved by the prayers of the local parishioners. The **Mývatn Nature Baths** are a northern version of the Blue Lagoon, but less touristy. The water is great for your skin, kept at 38–40°C (100–104°F), and there are several natural hotpots to try as well as massage areas, a natural steam bath and a café.

Mývatn Nature Baths: Jarðbaðshólar. Tel: 464 4411. www.jardbodin.is. Open: Jun–Aug daily 9am–midnight; Sept–May daily noon–10pm. Admission charge.

Laufás

A little way from Akureyri but still part of the Akureyri Museum, Laufás is a good example of a turf farm set in a wonderful meadowland overlooking Ayjafjörður. The farm is not as big as Glaumbær (*see pp92–3*) but has nine interconnecting chambers and two other buildings. At its maximum capacity it is considered to have housed 30 family and staff members. The farm site traces its heritage back to pagan times but the present structure dates from the 1850s to the 1880s, and has undergone an extensive renovation programme. The artefacts on display include work tools dating from around the turn of the 20th century.

Laufás: tel: 462 4162. www.akmus.is. Open: daily 9am–6pm. Admission charge.

The turf farm at Laufás

Siglufjörður

Out on a limb with a single road in and out, at the very top end of Iceland, you may be tempted to leave Siglufjörður out of the itinerary. But this is more than just another small fishing town and you would be missing one of Iceland's most fascinating museums: **Síldarminjasafnið** (Icelandic Herring-Era Museum). It won the European Museum of the Year award in 2004 and is centred on a turn-of-the-20th-century herring-salting factory called

Roaldsbrakki, where teams of herring-salting girls would descend in the summer season to gut, salt and pack the fish in wooden barrels in preparation for shipping. At peak production in 1916, 10,000 barrels of herring were salted. The building remained in use until 1968.

The rooms upstairs are a treasure-trove of everyday detail, from 1950s Hollywood pin-ups to hair rollers to nylon stockings drying over washing lines. Up to as many as 50 girls and women shared the kitchen and dorm-style bedrooms. However, they had little time for sleep as the season was short and the almost 24-hour daylight was used to its full advantage.

The ground floor of the 'brakki' was used as offices and the wages room is intact. The rest of the floor tells the story of herring in Iceland – of the good times when they arrived in their millions and the bad when they failed to arrive at all. Outside the building a herring boat stands in a faux harbour, as if just docking to land its catch. On Saturday afternoons from June to early August, salting demonstrations are held in front of the 'brakki'.

Those with an engineering bent will enjoy the neighbouring herring-processing shed that was purchased intact by the museum and which includes the coal- and dust-fired drying machines and the presses that extracted herring oil.

The final building is the most recent addition and is an excellent reproduction of the old quayside, complete with a genuine herring trawler and several smaller boats. There are wonderful photographs of Siglufjörður in its heyday. *Síldarminjasafnið: Hafn. Tel: 476 1604. www.sild.is. Open: Jun–Aug daily 10am–6pm; Sept–May daily 1–5pm. Admission charge.*

Take a trip back in time at the Icelandic Herring-Era Museum

Place names

Getting used to the pronunciation of place names is one of the most taxing jobs for a newly arrived visitor.

However, many of the towns and villages have very practical and historically relevant reasons for their names.

Let us start with the capital, Reykjavík. When the first settler Ingólfur Arnarson threw the wooden pillars that would be the foundation of his farmhouse into the sea and vowed to settle where they landed – a common Viking custom, he watched them float away around a headland and towards an area where smoke or steam was coming out of the ground. Ingólfur named his farm 'smoky harbour' or, in Icelandic, Reykjavík.

Most places, be they historic settler farms or more modern trader towns, were thus named for the geographical feature that defined their location. Many were named before a written language was introduced in Iceland, so the verbal connection to an actual landscape or to the people living in a place, such as 'past red crag peak and the deep inlet, just beyond X's farm', was the standard way to describe a place.

Remembering the meanings of some of these words will help you understand what sort of place you will find when you reach your destination.

Á – river
Alda – ridge of many hills or peaks
Bær – farm or small settlement

On the island of Heimæy, signs indicate the names of streets buried by a volcanic eruption in 1973

Bakki – riverbank
Brekka – slope or scree
Brú – bridge
Dalur – valley
Djúp – long inlet cut in from the coast
Eiði – isthmus
Ey – as the ending to a name means 'island' (plural *eyjar*)
Fell – hill
Fjall – mountain
Fjörður – broad inlet or fjord
Fljot – wide river
Foss – waterfall
Gil – gorge
Gja – fissure
Háls – ridge
Heiði – heath or moorland
Hlið – mountainside
Höfði – promontory
Höfn – harbour
Hóll – rounded hill (plural *hólar*)
Hólmur – small island or islet
Hraun – lava field
Hver – hot spring
Jökull – glacier
Jökulsá – glacial river
Kirkja – church
Klettur – cliff
Laug – warm spring
Múli – headland
Nes – headland or peninsula
Ós – estuary
Sandur – sands
Skagi – peninsula
Skard – mountain pass
Skógur – woodland or scrubland

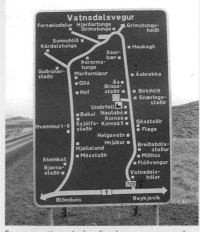

For non-natives, Icelandic place names can be tongue-twisters

Staður – parsonage
Stapi – crag
Tjörn – small lake
Vað – ford
Vatn – lake or water
Vegur – track
Vík – small inlet
Vellir – plains (singular *völlur*)
Vogur – inlet or creek

Lots of place names are simply a combination of descriptive words such as above. So Laugarbakki is 'the place of warm springs on the riverbank', or Kirkjufell is 'the church on, or by, the hill'. Of course, it gets a little hard to follow when it comes to Kirkjubæjarklauster or 'church, farm, cloister', but it is usually a simple 'where, why or who' as far as Icelandic place names are concerned.

Drive: West from Akureyri

This tour around the fjord west of Akureyri takes you through an expansive range of Iceland's attractions.

Time: 8 hours.

Distance: 360km (224 miles).

1 Akureyri Museum

This is the best of Akureyri's museums and galleries.

Leave the town by the ring road route 1 north. Where this cuts inland after 12km (7 miles), carry on along the fjordside road, route 82 to Dalvík.

2 The Hvoll Folk Museum, Dalvík

The Hvoll Folk Museum is a mixture of galleries celebrating industries and luminaries such as 'Jóhann the Giant', one of the tallest men ever.

Continue north along route 82. Just offshore, the island of Hrisey is always in view. You can take a ferry there from Dalvík.

3 Hrisey

Hrisey, a tiny island in the waters of the Eyjafjörður, is the largest offshore rock after Heimæy in the Westman Islands (*see pp128–31*). The island has been inhabited since early settlement days.

After 13km (8 miles), the road sweeps inland, and up and over the foothills of the Þverárjökull. It drops again to meet

the eastern coast of Skagafjörður and you will reach the junction with route 76. Turn right here for the 25km (16-mile) road into Siglufjörður.

4 Siglufjörður

Siglufjörður's *pièce de résistance* is the Icelandic Herring-Era Museum, a fly-on-the-wall look at what made the town great. This is not merely dry statistics but an exposition of how it really happened.

Return down route 76 and carry on past the junction with the 82. The road swings into Skagafjörður proper; after 35km (22 miles), you will find Hofsós on your left.

5 Hofsós

The harbour at Hofsós has one of the best collections of genuine and replica historic trader buildings in Iceland. Visit the Icelandic Emigration Centre to find out why so many people left the country for the New World and how they fared. On the outskirts of the town (on the left as you leave) you will see tiny Gröf, the oldest extant church in the country.

Carry on south on route 76 for around 14km (9 miles), where you will spot a turning left to Hólar.

6 Hólar Cathedral

Hólar Cathedral was one of two Catholic bishroprics before the Lutheran Reformation. The church building on the site today has an important altarpiece dating from the early 16th century.

Return to route 76 and turn left. At the junction of route 75 at the head of the fjord, turn right and keep the water on your right all the way to Sauðárkrókur.

7 Sauðárkrókur

Sauðárkrókur has a small museum on the harbourfront, and a blacksmith's still in its original condition.

Stay on route 75 south of Sauðárkrókur. After 18km (11 miles), you reach Glaumbær.

8 Glaumbær

Glaumbær is the largest turf farmhouse complex on the island at the Skagafjörður Folk Museum.

From the Skagafjörður Folk Museum, carry on south until you reach route 1, then turn left to Akureyri. You will reach the town after passing through 90km (56 miles) of exceptional upland glacial landscape including the Öxnadalsheiði and Öxnadalur valleys.

Drive: West from Akureyri

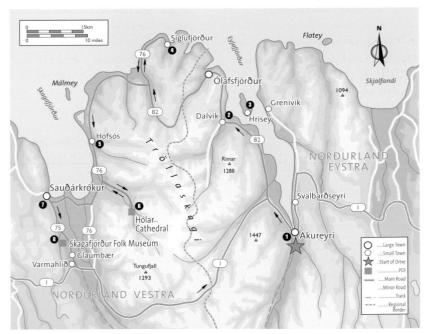

Drive: Around Lake Mývatn

Lake Mývatn, Iceland's fourth-largest lake, is a unique ecosystem with its volcanic parentage and geothermal fields. Watch out for the black fly, which makes a beeline for your mouth and nostrils. A handkerchief over the nose and mouth is useful but a head net is even better. There are also more species of duck here than anywhere in Europe, 15 in all.

Time: 5 hours. Distance: 40km (25 miles).

Start at the main town of Reykjahlíð.

1 Reykjahlíð

Reykjahlið parish church is set on ground surrounded by lava flows from the devastating 1783 eruption. The church was miraculously spared.

Leave the town heading west on route 87 in the direction of Húsavík through the dark lava. After 4km (2½ miles), turn left on route 848. At the junction is information relating to the ecosystem.

Lake Mývatn abounds with birdlife

2 Hrauneyjartjarnir and Hólmatjörn

This route weaves in through the Hrauneyjartjarnir and Hólmatjörn lava fields where many of the fissures have cracked and dropped. This has left abundant holes and small caves that are now lined with moss and so are ideal for nesting birds. This road may be closed during the nesting season.

After 11.5km (7 miles), the road crosses the Laxá River.

3 Laxá River

You will see many birds enjoying the oxygenated waters of the river here. Laxá means 'salmon' in Icelandic and these fish do spawn in the waters but only in the lower reaches closer to the sea.

200m (656ft) beyond the bridge, route 848 meets the junction with route 1. Turn left here to find the southern bank of the lake. After 5km (3 miles), you will find the Skutustaðir pseudo-crater park on the left. Stop here to take a stroll.

4 Skutustaðir

The Skutustaðagígar craters are small at around 20m (66ft) in height. The collection lies around Stakhólstjörn, a pond cut off from the lake.
Continue east along route 1. At Garður the road swings north and there are excellent views across the lake. After another 3km (2 miles), you will reach Hofði. Turn left into the car park.

5 Hofði

Hofði is a wooded basalt promontory that offers some of the most picturesque views of Mývatn. The forest consists of a mixture of birch and spruce.
Continue north for 3km (2 miles) to Dimmuborgir on the right.

6 Dimmuborgir

This lava field on the east side of the lake has some of the most intriguing and surreal lava pillars and cones.
Return to route 1 and continue north. After just over 1km (²⁄₃ mile), you will see a farm gate on the right with a sign for Hverfjall crater. Enter the gate but remember to close it behind you.

7 Hverfjall

Hverfjall crater is said to be the largest of its kind in the world. You can walk up the sides of this 'black' hill but stay on the paths because this is a very fragile landscape.
Return to route 1 and turn right. After 5.5km (3½ miles), you will find yourself back at Reykjahlíð.

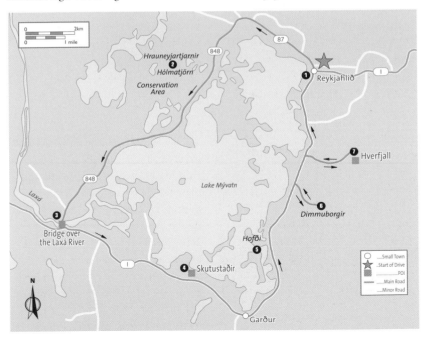

The anatomy of a volcano

Cracked lava flow

Iceland straddles the mid-Atlantic ridge – a 16,000km (9,944-mile) seam in the earth where the North American and Eurasian tectonic plates meet. This area is one of the most volcanically active in the world, with an eruption every five years or so. **Mount Katla** has erupted 20 times since records began in 1104, and **Hekla** 18 times. Scientists estimate that around one-third of the basaltic lavas that have flowed since medieval times have been produced by Icelandic eruptions.

Most of the plate activity in Iceland takes place as seamounts (underwater mountains) under the sea surface. These are created as the plates move apart, allowing hot molten rock or magma to reach the surface. However, volcanologists have concluded that in addition to plate activity, Iceland is also a location of hotspot (a very hot area under the earth's crust), further enhancing

volcanic potency. This hotspot is thought to be small but very deep, extending up to 650km (404 miles) into the earth's core.

Types of volcano

Volcanoes can be classed by the type of material that erupts.

Magma with low amounts of silica is called mafic. It is very fluid and travels great distances. This type is more common in Iceland. Iceland's þjórsárhraun mafic flow around 8,000 years ago covered 800sq km (309sq miles) and travelled a distance of 130km (81 miles).

Magma that contains a lot of silica is known as felsic. It is viscous and solidifies quickly but can cause sudden explosive eruptions because it blocks magma chambers, allowing pressure to rebuild inside the chamber.

Hverfjall volcanic crater

Kerið explosion crater

Iceland has many other indications of volcanic or hot-spot activity. The island experiences regular low-intensity earthquakes, has numerous natural hot springs (*see pp146–7 & pp116–17 for further information*), fumaroles (from where hot sulphurous gases escape from the earth's crust), boiling mud-pots (acidic hot springs coloured by melted mud) and geysers (super-heated water forced through a narrow opening to explode into the air).

Icelandic eruptions

1783 The largest lava flow yet recorded was at Laki when a row of craters spewed forth an estimated 13km³ (3 cubic miles) of molten rock. Livestock was poisoned by the gas and the sun was dulled by ash in the atmosphere, resulting in a famine that killed 10,000 people.

1963 A submarine eruption on the Reykjanes ridge off southwestern Iceland spawned the island of Surtsey. This virgin land was thrust 130m (427ft) up from the sea floor and had an area of almost 3sq km (1sq mile).

1973 The volcanic site of Eldfell on Heimæy appeared out of the blue. The eruption lasted for five months and was a classic sight, spewing molten lava and caustic ash. The lava threatened to cut off the town's harbour from the sea.

1996 The Grímsvötn volcano erupted underneath the Vatnajökull glacier, melting thousands of cubic metres of ice. This was released in a *jökulhlaup* (catastrophic flood caused by the ice-wall giving way, allowing a sudden release of melted water). 1.14km³ (¼ cubic mile) of water swept across the *sandur* carrying with it roads and bridges.

2000 Hekla: a 4.5km (2¾-mile) fissure sent ash several kilometres up into the air.

2004 Grímsvötn erupted once again with a steam plume rising several kilometres into the air.

2010 In April, a small volcano under Eyjafjallajökull glacier in southern Iceland erupted. The surrounding population was evacuated for fear that the volcano would trigger nearby Mount Katla and cause a catastrophic *jökulhlaup*. Ash produced by the volcano grounded flights across Europe in the largest flight grounding since 9/11.

Eastern Iceland coast and highlands

Iceland's eastern fjords are totally different in geography from those in the west. With high slender peaks rather than plateau summits, the road hugs the water's edge at their base, and the several tiny settlements are strung along it like pearls on a string.

In many ways, the towns of the Eastfjords take second place to their surrounding landscape and spectacular setting. Access routes up and over mountain passes offer panoramic views down the deep coastal inlets, while sea-level vantage points lead the eye to sweeping scree slopes and jagged peaks complemented by colourful reflections in the languid waters.

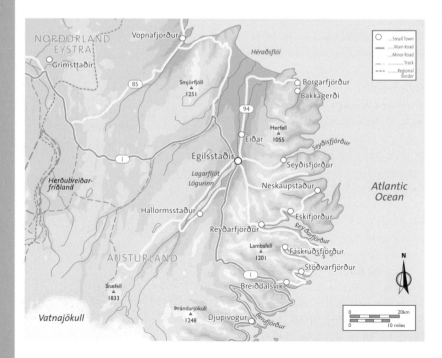

THE CREATURE OF LAGARFLJÓT

Just like Loch Ness in Scotland, Lagarfljót is said to have its own monster, Lagarfljótsormurinn. This huge marine creature is only rarely seen and has never been witnessed by scientists or recorded on sonar devices or video cameras. It's often called the Iceland Worm Monster and is presumed to be longer than a football pitch. It can apparently slither on land, and sightings have been consistently logged since 1345. There are many reports of supernatural events in Lagarfljót, possibly connected to gases forced up out of the water.

Fishing is king here, with every fjord having its own processing plant. The towns are also fiercely proud of their heritage and each has a small museum of some kind or another. If you are touring this area, the route means you will be passing through most of them – so take your pick.

Djúpivogur

The oldest trading post in the region with a history dating back to the 16th century, Djúpivogur now has a population of just under 500 people. The cultural centre of the town is **Langa-Buð** (1790), once the town store and now a combined museum/gallery, information centre and café. In the wild areas east of the village, you should see seals and seabirds on the rocks.

From the harbour regular summer ferries run to **Papey** (Friar's) Island where the early Irish monk settlers founded a hermitage. Today, it is a haven for hikers with a small wooden church and a lighthouse. You will have only nesting seabirds for company. Guided trips, seal and birdwatching trips and harbour tours are on offer.
Langa-Buð: Buð 1. Tel: 478 8288. www.djupivogur.is. Open: Jun–Aug daily 10am–6pm. Admission charge to museum.

Egilsstaðir

Eastern Iceland's main town sits inland from the coast. There is little charm about the place itself but it is a base from which to explore the surrounding area and to take a boat trip on **Lagarfljót**, a substantial river that forms a long slim lake, **Lögurinn**, to the northwest of town.

The harbour at Djúpivogur

A small café in Fáskrúðsfjörður

Egilsstaðir's **Minjasafn Austurlands** heritage museum explains the history and development of the region and includes some interesting Viking jewellery and other pagan artefacts found at nearby Þórisá plus re-creations of rooms in a traditional farm.

The controversial **Kárahnjúkar Dam** feeds power to the aluminium smelting plant constructed inland from the head of the lake just southwest of Egilsstaðir. The Visitor Centre offers more information about the whole project, which has become a tourist attraction. *Minjasafn Austurlands: Laufskógar 1. Tel: 471 1412. www.minjasafn.is.*

Open: Jun–Aug daily 11am–5pm; Sept–May Mon–Fri 1–5pm. Admission charge. Lake trip on Lagarfljótsormurinn cruise ship: From the bridge at Fellabær. Tel: 471 2900. Times change with season. Admission charge. Kárahnjúkar Dam Visitor Centre: Végarður. Tel: 471 2044. www.karahnjukar.is. Open: May–Sept daily 9am–5pm. Free admission.

Eskifjörður

Set in its own inner fjord on the larger Reyðarfjörður, Eskifjörður plays host to the **Sjominjasafn Austurlands** (East Iceland's Maritime Museum). Set in an old warehouse, Gamla-Buð, dating from 1816, the museum showcases the importance of fishing to the region over the last two centuries, including details of the shark-fishing and whaling industries. The old town's general store is also re-created here.
Sjominjasafn Austurlands: Stradgata 39b. Tel: 470 9063. Open: Jun–Aug daily 1–5pm; Sept–May by arrangement. Admission charge.

Fáskrúðsfjörður

Fáskrúðsfjörður was settled by French sailors in the late 1800s when they used this fjord as a base for their fishing trips. The tiny museum, **Fransmenn á Íslandi** (French Fishermen in Iceland), explores the history of the sailors until their final departure in 1914, from their fishing disasters to the close diplomatic relations that developed between the two countries. A small cemetery along the shoreline is the resting place for those who did not return to France. The street signs are in both Icelandic and French in remembrance of the town's foreign 'brothers'.

Fransmenn á Íslandi: Búðavegi 8. Tel: 475 1525. www.sjominjar.is. Open: daily 10am–6pm. Admission charge.

Hallormsstaður

Iceland's largest forest sits on the southern bank of the Lagarfljót close to Egilsstaðir. The 800-hectare (1,977-acre) tract was the private domain of Iceland's publishing magnate, Guðmundur Magnússon, in the 18th century. He began the planting of native deciduous species such as birch, ash and Alaskan poplar, a process that is now managed by the Iceland Forestry Commission.

Open access.

Neskaupstaður

Home of one of Iceland's largest fish processing plants, Neskaupstaður benefited from the herring boom in the 1920s. The **Náttúrugripasanið** (Natural History Museum) does not have nearly as many examples of rocks and minerals as Steinasafn Petru (*see p115*) but **Tryggvasafn** (the Tryggvi Gallery) is worth a detour if you enjoy modern art. Local son Tryggvi Ólafsson is one of Iceland's leading lights.

Once again, it is probably the journey to the town, over the hills in the lee of **Mount Hólafjall** from Eskifjörður, that

makes it worthwhile going there.

Náttúrugripasanið: Miðstræti 1. Tel: 477 1454. Open: Jun–Aug daily 1–5pm; Sept–May by arrangement. Admission charge.

Tryggvasafn: Hafnarbraut 2. Tel: 861 4747. www.fjardabyggd.is. Open: Jun–Aug daily 2–5pm; Sept–May by arrangement. Admission charge.

Reyðarfjörður

Reyðarfjörður is one of eastern Iceland's newest settlements. It was not established until the 20th century but its sheltered position at the head of the longest fjord in the region brought it to notice during World War II when it played host to an important military base. British forces arrived in 1940 and a Norwegian air force squadron was billeted here in 1942.

Today, the small and rather eclectic **Íslenzka stríðsárasafnið** (Icelandic Wartime Museum) commemorates the war years. It is sited in the 1940s Spítalakampur that was part of the original complex.

Inland from the head of Reyðarfjörður is the site of the controversial Alcoa aluminium smelting plant. It has made the town one of the busiest and most prosperous along the coast.

Íslenzka stríðsárasafnið: Spítalakampi near Hæðargerði. Tel: 470 9095. Open: Jun–Aug daily 1–5pm. Admission charge.

Seyðisfjörður

The cultural centre of the Eastfjords, Seyðisfjörður has a music school and welcomes many Icelandic artists during the summer. When the Smyril Lines ferry from Denmark docks it gets as busy as Reykjavík and this link ensures its economic buoyancy.

The town was founded in the mid-19th century by Norwegian businessmen and developed on the back of herring fishing. As their wealth grew, they began importing wooden 'kit' homes from Norway. At the end of the century Otto Wathne was the most prominent of these businessmen – he is known as the father of the town and his plant, Angró, was built in 1881.

In 1906, the fjord was chosen as the entry point for Iceland's submarine telephone cable – a new link with the outside world. The telegraph company brought new ideas and a new period of prosperity.

Today, Seyðisfjörður is one of the most architecturally interesting of Iceland's towns with a wealth of period buildings dating from the late 18th and early 19th centuries (*see pp118–19*), when the town was in its heyday.

Tækniminjasafn Austurlands (Technical Museum for East Iceland) celebrates Wathne's legacy and the coming of telecommunications in a group of several buildings including machine shops that will please anyone with an interest in engineering, the old telegraph station and the Wathne mansion built in 1894. Stop at the top of the one-way out road to Seyðisfjörður for exceptional panoramic views of the town hundreds of metres below at the head of its thread-like fjord.

Tækniminjasafn Austurlands: Hafnargata 44. Tel: 472 1596. www.tekmus.is. Open: Jun–mid-Sept daily 11am–5pm; mid-Sept–May

A view of Seyðisfjörður with its stave church and lovely period buildings

Mon–Fri 1–4pm; other times by arrangement. Admission charge.

Stöðvarfjörður

This is home to one of Iceland's most unusual museums, **Steinasafn Petru** (Petra's Stone Collection), a collection of thousands of rocks and minerals gathered over 70 years by a local woman, Petra Sveinsdóttir. The small house and garden are crammed with examples small and large, and include agates, zeolites and semi-precious stones. *Steinasafn Petru: Sunnuhulið. Tel: 755 8834. Open: daily 9am–6pm. Admission charge.*

Vopnafjörður to Borgarfjörður

The ride into Vopnafjörður is the main attraction, though the setting of this small northern town is pretty enough. Up and over the Hauksstaðaheiði from Akureyri or along the switchback incline of the mountains to the south, the views are some of the most dramatic in the Eastfjords.

Take the switchback for equally impressive views over Héraðssandur, the languid delta of the Jökulsá á Dal and Lagerfljót Rivers, which is a major birdwatching area. Just south of Héraðssandur is a small inlet, Borgarfjörður, where the artist Jóhannes Kjarval spent his childhood and found his inspiration. **Kjarvalsstofa** (the Kjarval Experience) is this rural community's tribute to their most famous son. It displays some reproductions of his works and acts as an education centre. Kjarval painted the altarpiece of the nearby Baggaverði Church.

If you are flying from Reykjavík to Egilsstaðir, it is also possible to hire a car at the airport and drive around the region. Without a car, you can also travel from Egilsstaðir directly to Borgarfjörður in the Jakob and Margret's postal van (*see Tourist Information in Egilsstaðir for the times and contact number*). The area around Borgarfjörður is rich with hiking possibilities. Organised tours can be arranged, allowing you to hike from place to place while your baggage is transported to the next guesthouse where you will be staying.

If you do not have time to travel to the Westman Islands to see the puffins, you can enjoy discovering puffins, eider ducks, kittiwakes, fulmars, guillemots and razorbills who nest from June to August in Hafnarbjarg, 3km (2 miles) east of Borgarfjörður. A birdwatcher platform has been built and is accessible every day (*10am–10pm*) at no charge. There are modest guesthouses in the rough and rural area by the ocean.

This is Iceland in its purest form. For information about Egilsstaðir, contact the tourist office at *east@east.is*, or *www.east.is*
Kjarvalsstofa: Borgarfirði Eystra (Community Centre). Tel: 472 9950. Open: Jun–Aug daily 11am–5pm; Sept–May daily 1–5pm. Admission charge.

The green issue

Iceland stands square at the heart of the green dilemma. It is one of the least polluted countries on earth and takes full advantage of what nature has provided. On the one hand, it is fêted as a forward-thinking example to the rest of the world, but it is also taking decisions that are unpopular with the international community, largely dictated by its economy.

The pluses
Keeping warm Geothermal heat is one of Iceland's advantages. Inexpensive and reliable, it does not add to the world's problems of global warming or carbon dioxide emissions. The first attempts in Iceland to capture power directly from Mother Earth were as early as 1755, but a concerted attempt began in 1928 when the first boreholes were drilled to harness the hot water beneath Reykjavík. Today, 90 per cent of Iceland's houses have geothermal heat and you will never be short of hot (sulphurous-smelling) water for your morning shower.

Ecotourism Much of the appeal of Iceland stems from its natural abundance and the country has not been slow in seeing the economic possibilities, including whale-watching expeditions from around the island, puffin-spotting – though with two million birds around Iceland one would think you'd be falling over them in the streets – glacier tours and volcano hikes. Hiking, cycling and horse riding are eco-friendly and popular ways of getting around.

The minuses
The aluminium industry
The Kárahnjúkar Dam in Iceland has caused much controversy. Located in Europe's second-largest, formerly unspoilt, wilderness, it uses rivers from part of Europe's largest glacier, Vatnajökull. Sigur Rós and Björk were among many high-profile activists against the project in the late 2000s. At Reyðarfjörður (see p113), there is an aluminium smelting plant that has dammed a major river valley. This caused an enormous change in the landscape and ecosystem of one of the most remote and unspoilt parts of the country.

Polls conducted by the Institute of Social Sciences, University of Iceland, and the well-respected Gallup show that over 64 per cent of Icelanders approved of the plants. In Reykjavík fewer people were happy about it but in the countryside around 75 per cent said yes. The allure is the 1,200 jobs that the plants will create, in a part of the island that is losing people to migration because of lack of employment.

Whaling In 2003, Iceland's government approved a plan to restart whale hunting after a hiatus of over a decade. Ironically, the country had come late to commercial whaling, leaving the trade to the Norwegians on Icelandic soil until late into the 20th century. It continues today and, in 2010, Iceland defied the International Whaling Commission, saying it would leave the committee if it was restricted further in its whaling. It currently has a quota for 100 minke whales and 150 fin whales. Environmentalists have been outraged, but should Iceland be forced to join the EU for economic reasons, it will have to give up whaling as a condition of membership.

Back in 2004, the minister for fisheries, Arni Mathieson, said in a speech that since the country was 'overwhelmingly dependent on the utilisation of living marine resources', it would continue to kill whales for scientific purposes but that only the minke species would be involved – Norway, Japan and Russia have been criticised for their whaling, and now Iceland is again under fire from conservationists. The controversial research is said to focus on the role of whales in the marine ecosystem and to be economically sustainable because the whale products are sold in the world market – though only Japan has a demand for such products.

Icelanders tend to be pro-whaling but, following a historic gig, Náttúra, by Björk and Sigur Rós in Reykjavík in 2008, there is a growing environmentally conscious movement.

Iceland benefits from geothermal power generation

Walk: Seyðisfjörður

Founded in the mid-19th century by Norwegian entrepreneurs, Seyðisfjörður became one of the most successful trading towns in Iceland. As the money rolled in, these families began to live in beautiful houses, many of which were ordered from a catalogue and shipped from Scandinavia. This walk features a few important examples.

Time: 2½ hours with museum visit.

Distance: 1.5km (1 mile).

Start at the church on Bjólfsgata.

1 Bjólfsgata Church

The church was originally built further down the fjord but was blown off its foundations and rebuilt here in 1922.
Cross Bjólfsgata and walk down Norðgata.

2 Norðgata

The buildings here make for an ensemble of Norwegian imports: the Framtið village store (1920), Lárahús (1899), the post office (1903) and the 1901 Magasíníð, which is now used as a cobbler's workshop.
Turn right at the end of Norðgata and walk a short way along Vesturvegur; and look for No 7 on the left.

3 Vesturvegur – No 7

This is the oldest concrete building in the town, built in 1899.
Return to the intersection with Norðgata, turn right and cross the Fjarðará River. Immediately on your right is Suðurgata. Stop at the first building on the right.

4 Suðurgata

Suðurgata was originally at the entrance of the drive to a hospital that was constructed in 1898. This first building on the right was the pharmacy.
Return to the main road, Austurvegur, and turn right, keeping the fjord on your left. You will pass four colourful cottages on your left. Stop at Austurvegur 9.

5 Austurvegur 9 – Ós

Ós was originally the station house near the water's edge for the old ferry that used to take passengers across the head of the fjord before the bridge was built. The present house dates from 1907 and was built in the same style as the imported Norwegian houses.
Continue along Austurvegur.

6 Steinholt

Standing alone on the right is Steinholt. Built in 1907, it is the home of Iceland's renowned music school.

Austurvegur bears right once you have crossed the next intersection. Climb the slight incline to the first house on the right.

7 Einsdæmi

This is a corrugated-iron-clad building from 1907, home of Iceland's first female MP, Arnbjörg Sveinsdóttir.
Further up on the same side is Skaftafell.

8 Skaftafell

Built in 1907 as a restaurant and guesthouse by goldsmith Bjarni Sigursson, the building is now the Seyðisfjörður's arts centre.
Continue along Austurvegur until you come to Fossgata on the right. Turn up here to Járnhúsið.

9 Járnhúsið

Járnhúsið was the first iron-framed building in Iceland.
Return to Austurvegur and turn right. You will almost immediately come to the intersection with Hafnargata (Harbour Street) and you will walk into what used to be the business end of town in the late 1880s. At the end of the town is the Technical Museum for East Iceland.

10 Technical Museum for East Iceland

The museum comprises several buildings, including Otto Wathne's fish processing plant (1881) and the Wathne family mansion (1894), purchased by the Icelandic Telephone Company with the coming of the undersea cable.

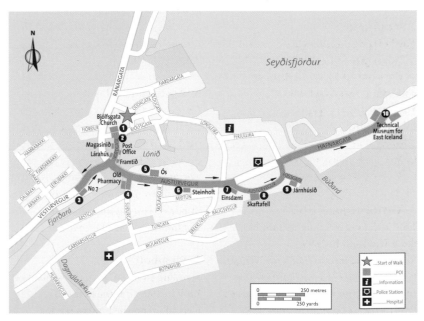

Southern Iceland

The south of the country is Iceland at its most intense, marked by brooding volcanoes (some still active), vast glaciers and a puffin bonanza every summer. Tour buses ply the route daily from Reykjavík but they only scratch the surface. Hire a car to explore it to the full. The attractions here demand a stay of a few days, even if only to take in the sheer power of nature stored here.

Dyrhólæy

This small wedge-shaped headland's name means 'doorway hill island', and it is taken from a stone arch protruding from its southern tip that is large enough for a sizeable boat to pass through. The cliffs around 'the doorway' rise vertically to 120m (394ft) with many caves and stacks. It is a favourite nesting place for seabirds.

On the landward side, Dyrhólæy protects a shallow coastal lagoon that is

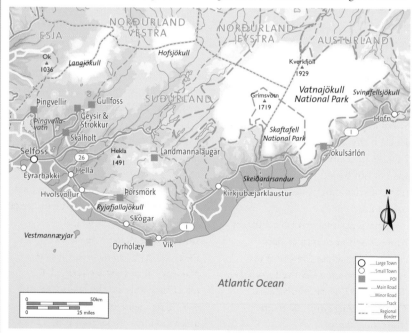

Atlantic Ocean

○	Large Town
○	Small Town
■	POI
—	Main Road
—	Minor Road
- · -	Track
-··-	Regional Border

a favourite roosting spot for eiders, swans and wading birds. The grassy slopes of the leeward side offer the perfect habitat for ground-nesting species. So, all in all, this is one of the best sites for birdwatching and has been designated a nature reserve. You can drive up to a couple of car parks for excellent views of the cliffs from up close (if it's not the nesting season), or park at the entrance and enjoy the walk (see pp134–5).

Dyrhólæyjarferðir. Tel: 487 8500. www.dyrholaey.com. Amphibious tours around the rocks at the site summer daily.

The cliffs of Dyrhólæy

Hekla

Brooding Hekla rises above the Vesturlandejar and Austurlandejar plains, casting a long shadow over southern Iceland. Her cold white mantle hides a molten heart and this volcano has been responsible for some of the worst eruptions in Iceland's recorded history including the most damaging one in 1104 that swallowed farms and villages within a radius of 50km (31 miles). In popular myth, Hekla is the doorway to hell, a red-hot keyhole into everlasting agony. Her last gasp of hot breath was in 2000, and a team of seismologists takes readings round the clock.

There is an information centre on route 26 with exhibitions and explanations about the volcano. *Hekla Information Centre: Leirubakki. Tel: 487 6587. www.leirubakki.is. Open: Jun–Aug daily 10am–6pm. Admission charge.*

Höfn

Geographically, Höfn (pronounced like a shortened 'hope') is in eastern Iceland, but since its attractions relate to its proximity to the Vatnajökull volcano, it features in the southern Iceland section instead.

Until the building of the ring road, the town was as remote as you could get from Reykjavík as you had to travel west through Akureyri to reach the capital. That was because the Skeiðarársandur was impassable. Today, it is a sizeable if bland settlement, a commercial centre for the surrounding crofters and a commercial fishing port. Most visitors pass through for its range of eateries and for its **Ísland Jöklasýning** (Glacier Exhibition). Everything you need to know about glaciers – how they are formed, the effect they have on the landscape and the current state of health of glacial areas vis-à-vis global warming – can be found here. There is also an interesting video show about the last great Grímsvötn eruption and the effect that it had on the area. Many of the interesting glacial features along the ring road are signposted with the Glacier Exhibition logo.

Höfn has a couple of other museums that you can visit if the Glacier Exhibition has not filled you with an immediate desire to head out to Vatnajökull. **Gamla buð**, a mid-19th-century warehouse, is the oldest building in Höfn, dating to 1864, now operating as a folk museum and museum of natural history.

Ísland Jöklasýning: Hafnarbraut 30. Tel: 478 2665. Open: Jun–Aug daily 9am–10pm; May & Sept daily 1–6pm & 8–10pm. Special openings can be requested outside regular opening hours. Admission charge.
Gamla buð: Litlabrú 2. Tel: 470 8050.

Jökulsárlón – a glacial lagoon

Open: Jun 2–6pm; Jul–Aug 2–8pm; open on request in winter.
Admission charge.

Jökulsárlón (Glacier Lagoon)

Another of nature's wonders, 350km (217 miles) east of Reykjavík, Jökulsárlón is one of the most photographed landscapes in Iceland and the venue (with computer enhancements) for the ice-race scenes in James Bond's *Die Another Day*. Jökulsárlón is an iceberg lagoon and Breiðamerkurjökull's outlet to the sea.

Hundreds of these blue-white leviathans float silently in the limpid waters. In the distance beyond, the cold blue tongue of the glacier can be seen from the shore and from the main coast road that crosses the lagoon's mouth. Half-hour boat trips head out through the icy maze for an intimate encounter that contains the secrets of millennia, but they are pricey and most sights can be seen from the shore.

Boat trips: 20–30 minutes from the car park at the site. Tel: 478 2122. www.jokulsarlon.com.
Rides: 10am–5pm depending on numbers. Admission charge.

Kirkjubæjarklaustur

This almost unpronounceable name, meaning 'church, farm, convent', is usually shortened to 'Klaustur'. The village sits on the southern borders of Skeiðarársandur. There is not much more here than a fuel station and hotel, though, as its name suggests, it was an important Catholic centre before the Reformation. Many of the surrounding hills and rock formations have names that hark back to the religious community that had a home here.

A couple of hundred metres out of the village you'll find **Kirkjugólf** (church floor), a series of natural basalt columns whose ends have been worn away to resemble a man-made tiled floor, thought to be the remains of an old church.

Kirkugólf: open access. Free admission.

Landmannalaugar

Landmannalaugar sits in the heart of some of Iceland's most evocative landscapes – the red, gold and bronze hues of the rhyolite rocks that seem almost unreal in their intensity, especially when the sun is low in the sky shining its warmest light, geothermal pools, the highest geothermal field in the country, and upland valleys graced by lakes and streams.

The region around the lodge has some of the finest hiking and trekking routes in Iceland with some unforgettable views. If you don't have a booking to stay here, camping is your only other option.

Landmannalaugar's thermal pool is an unforgettable experience – a cold stream flows in and meets a hot geothermal stream, creating the perfect temperature. Day trips are available from Reykjavík; it is also the start or finish point for Iceland's great Landmannalaugar to Þórsmörk hiking trail (*see p126*).

Basalt blocks in Kirkjugólf

Skeiðarársandur

Iceland's largest glacial volcanic flood plain is also the world's largest, spreading southeast from the Vatnajökull basin to the Atlantic Ocean. An ever-shifting carpet of meltwater streams and soft alluvial sediment, it has always been one of Iceland's most mysterious regions, little understood till the arrival of volcanology.

Today, scientists can tell why the Skeiðarársandur looks like it does and how it was formed (by *jökulhlaup*, or a massive release of glacial meltwater due to volcanic eruption; *see pp10–11*), but cannot explain the strange beauty of the lifeless plain of gold and grey sand in the ever-changing colours of an Icelandic day.

It was common for Icelanders to gather stones to bring them good luck as they crossed the *sandur* and this

The impressive cascade of the Skógafoss

tradition is continued here. When the road was built many piles of stones would have been destroyed but they were collected by the highways department staff and placed in one location around a small pseudo-crater called **Laufskálavarða** (between Klausters and Vík), the site of a farm destroyed in an eruption as early as 894. Place your own stone here and you would be adding your bit to this very Icelandic custom.

Look out also for a memorial to the 1996 *jökulhlaup* on the main road just before Skaftafell National Park.

Skógar

The first thing you will notice as you approach Skógar is **Skógafoss**. This 60m (197ft) cascade is an impressive sight as it falls in a pure white curtain of foam; from either the summit or the base it is an excellent photo opportunity. Legend has it that there is treasure hidden behind the falls.

The other reason to pull off the main road into the village is **Skógasafn** (Skógar Folk Museum). Like many of Iceland's museums, the impetus for this folk museum was provided by a single individual who wanted to preserve memories of the old ways of life in the region.

The farm at Skógar used to be the nucleus of the collection, set on the coastal plain nestled in the shadow of the Skógaheiði hills and within the soothing sound of Skógafoss. The collection of wood-framed turf and stone buildings, dating from between 1830 and 1895, are equipped as though the farmer might return at any moment.

The museum expanded as the owner found many more buildings to rescue; he restored them and placed them behind the farm to create a sort of pseudo-village. There is a school built in 1901, a church, and Skál, a second farmhouse dating from the 1920s, all painstakingly returned to their original condition. The collection of artefacts in the museum is almost beyond belief. Not a thing seems to have slipped through the net, from the finest house to the humblest shack – furniture, clothing, bedding and decorative items cram the galleries. Downstairs there is a natural history section with birds' eggs, butterflies and insects stuck with pins – a Victorian gentleman's dream. The museum's most prized possession is an 1855 open fishing boat, which was in use until just after World War II.

An old fishing boat exhibit at Skógasafn

The **Samgöngusafnið** (Museum of Transport) explores the history of transport, communications and technology in Iceland in the 19th and 20th centuries. Early snowploughs and attempts at amphibious craft look the strangest, and lorries, tractors and family cars show the development over the decades.

Skógasafn: Hvolsvöllur.
Tel: 487 8845. www.skogasafn.is.
Open: Jun–Aug daily 9am–6pm; May &
Sept daily 10am–5pm; Oct–Apr daily
11am–4pm. Admission charge.

Þórsmörk

Surrounded by no fewer than three glaciers, the high valley of Þórsmörk is a hidden world and can only be reached by a 4WD or special vehicle. The high alpine scenery is worth the effort with numerous miniature canyons and cols (a saddle between two rocky ridges at the lowest point of a connection between two peaks), and fingers of ice extending down into the meltwater lake of Markarfljót. The ride across rivers and streams and past azure glacial lagoons is also pretty exciting.

Þórsmörk, meaning 'Thor's wood', is so named because the original settlers believed their God of War had a kind of holiday home here. Because of its pagan heritage, the valley is popular with Icelanders, who come to spend long summer days and particularly the summer solstice, considered a magical time for the Norse.

Southern Iceland

The 53km (33-mile) Laugarvegurinn walking route between Þórsmörk and Landmannalaugar (*see p123*) has become one of Iceland's most iconic walks. Through it you pass by glaciers, hot springs and mountains of every colour. It takes approximately four days. Walking routes near Fimmvörðuhals and the Eyjafjallajökull volcano have changed – consult the tourist office for up-to-date safe routes. Buses run between Landmannalaugar and Þórsmörk and Reykjavík five times daily mid-June–mid-September. Maps are available in Reykjavík.

Vatnajökull National Park

In 2008, the Vatnajökull glacier plus the two surrounding national parks were declared Europe's largest national park.

Skaftafell

Skaftafell protects over 1,700sq km (656sq miles) of Iceland's most typical upland landscape, including a large section of southern Vatnajökull, the **Grímsvötn volcano** and **Mount Grimsfjall**. Much of this land is inaccessible but the southernmost strip, where glacier meets rock, is one of the most visited locations. It is famous for its majestic vistas and its many accessible walks.

Skaftafelljökull protrudes down close to the national park office, and the rather untidy and dirty black tongue of the glacier sees an almost never-

The Vatnajökull glacier rests on an active volcano

Svinafellsjökull glacier (at the northeast of Vatnajökull National Park) is a majestic sight

ending parade of visitors. The same is true of **Svartifoss**, or Black Falls, named so not for the colour of the water but for the black basalt column that the cascade drops over. It is possible to walk down to the base and behind the water.

Skaftafell is not just about the macro-landscape; it is as much about smaller elements such as species of flora that flourish because sheep and horses are not allowed to graze here. In summer, there is a colourful population of butterflies and ground-nesting birds.

Skaftafell was the site of a large farm and a regional Þing (assembly) in the 13th century, located on the flat land at the base of the hills. However, the encroaching Skeiðarársandur forced the farmer to rebuild 100m (328ft) up the hill in the mid-19th century.

There are some excellent, well-marked walking routes up and beyond Svartifoss (*see pp132–3*).
National Park Headquarters:
tel: 470 8300.

www.vatnajokulsthjodgardur.is.
Open: hours vary from 8–11am until
3–9pm, depending on the month.

Vatnajökull

Iceland's most celebrated glacier casts its eye over much of the eastern coast. A vast white cape with many smaller subsidiary ice flows (including Breiðamerkurjökull, the flow that feeds Jökulsárlón and Fjallsjökull), it rests upon one of the world's most active volcanoes, Grímsvötn.

Meltwater from Vatnajökull caused the latest *jökulhlaup* across Skeiðarársandur (*see pp123–4*) during the 1996 eruption – a scientist's dream but a road engineer's nightmare, as miles of black-topped two-lane surfaces were carried away into the icy seas by the sudden wall of water. You can get

Svartifoss, or Black Falls, with its distinctive basalt columns

THE WESTMAN ISLANDS ERUPTION

On 23 January 1973, in the middle of the night, a violent volcanic eruption woke the people of these islands from their beds. Lava spewed from a new fissure, threatening their homes. Luckily, because of the bad weather that day the fishing fleet had not set sail from the harbour, and the 5,000 islanders were quickly evacuated by boat to the mainland.

The eruption continued and in March the magma threatened the harbour – the economic heart of the community. An emergency action plan to halt the flow by pumping millions of litres of icy seawater on to it worked well. All this happened under media spotlights as news crews around the world reported every twist and turn in the story. By the end of the episode in early July, over 300 houses had been lost but the harbour was saved.

up close on a snowmobile or other types of glacier tours – trips take about three hours.
Vatnajökull Tours: Vagnsstaðir. Tel: 478 1000. www.glacierjeeps.is

Vestmannæyjar (The Westman Islands)

A collection of small islands off the south coast of Iceland, the Westman Islands became world famous during the volcanic eruption of 1973 (*see box above*). Named so because in the 11th century they were home to a small group of renegade Irishmen, or 'men from the west', only one of the group of 16 islands, Heimæy, is inhabited. Apart from its reputation as a volcanic hotspot, life is quiet and uncomplicated here. The islanders make a living from

A volcanic sand beach on Heimæy

the sea – the fish within it or the birds that fly above it, including millions of migratory birds that arrive to nest on the cliffs of these islands. The economic harvest has always been in the meat and eggs of these birds, particularly puffins, which are considered a delicacy. Today, the traditional industries are supplemented by running whale- and puffin-watching trips for tourists.

The town has a handful of minor museums. **Byggðasafn** (Folk Museum) gives information about the island's history and development including a section on the eruption; **Landlyst** is a small museum housed in the old maternity hospital in a fort built by the English in the 15th century. There is also the small **Náttúrugripasafn** (Natural History Museum) with a collection of Icelandic fish and dioramas with stuffed native animals.

But getting out on to the footpaths of the island is the real reason for being here. It is the best way to view the nest sites – the puffins spend time on land only to nest, June to September. Sea tours from the islands can reveal groups of Orca and other whales. Another interesting trip is the route up the new volcanic cone **Eldfell**.

Visit the island in season (mid-August) and you can experience the 'Flight of the Puffling'. Thousands of fledging birds become disoriented

A hillside farm near Vík

by the lights of the town and fall ignominiously into the streets. Armed with a cardboard box and some soft fabric – a towel would do – you patrol the streets looking for them; carefully put them in the box and cover with the towel to keep them calm. The following morning the young birds are released on to the water to allow them to begin their journey to adulthood.

Westman Films runs regular shows on the volcanic eruption, the birth of neighbouring Surtsey Island, whale-watching and puffins.
Tourist office:
www.visitwestmanislands.com.
Byggðasafn: Ráðhústræti.
Tel: 481 1194. Open:
mid-May–mid-Sept daily 11am–5pm;
mid-Sept–mid-May Sat–Sun 3–5pm &

by arrangement. Admission charge.
Náttúrugripasafn: Heiðarvegur 12.
Tel: 481 1997. Open: May–mid-Sept
daily 11am–5pm; mid-Sept–May
Sat–Sun 3–5pm. Admission charge.
Puffin- and whale-watching: Viking
Tours. Suðurgerði 4. Tel: 488 4884.
www.vikingtours.is.
Volcano film show: Heiðarvegur.
Tel: 481 1045. Shows in English mid-
Jun–mid-Sept several times daily;
mid-Sept–mid-Jun by arrangement.
Admission charge.

The Westmans can be reached by ferry from Þórlákshöfn, though a new harbour is under construction in southern Iceland near Bakkafjara (*Herjólfur. Tel: 481 2800.*
www.herjolfur.is); or by air on a scheduled flight from Reykjavík city

airport (*Tel: 570 3030.*
www.airiceland.is), or by chartered
summer flights from Selfoss, Hella or
Bakki (*Tel: 481 3255. www.eyjaflug.is*).

Vík (í Mýrdal)

Birds flock to the basalt cliffs around
Vík í Mýrdal (always shortened to Vík)
and now tourists follow, to enjoy the
impressive offshore stacks and one of
the finest black volcanic beaches

anywhere. Offshore, the Reynisdrangar
Needles have long been a navigation
point on shipping charts.

Brydebuð, the old store, was built on
the Westman Islands in 1831 and
transported here in 1895. It is the oldest
timber house in this part of Iceland and
now hosts the tourist office and a small
maritime museum. On the same street
are a number of other gaily painted
houses and cottages.

The cliffs near Vík shelter numerous seabirds

Walk: Vatnajökull National Park

Vatnajökull National Park is most famous for its glaciers and volcanoes, but the southern tip around Skaftafell National Park has some wonderful verdant walking trails. In this itinerary we have linked some of the park's easy-to-reach attractions, though we would still recommend hardy shoes because the paths are uneven in places.

Time: 3 hours. Distance: 6km (3¾ miles).

Start at the National Park information building in Skaftafell. There is a large car parking area here.

1 National Park Visitor Centre

Before exploring the three different areas of Europe's largest national park, created in 2008 by combining Vatnajökull plus the two surrounding national parks, stop at the Visitor Centre to learn more about the history of the region and the way in which the forces of nature have formed it.

You can get a brochure and full-scale maps for longer excursions and pick up souvenir books of the region – though it may be best to leave this until after the walk since you don't want to carry too much weight.
Tel: 470 8300.
www.vatnajokulsthjodgardun.is. Opening hours vary according to the month.
Set out right from the Visitor Centre entrance and walk through the campsite along flat ground. Once past the site, the ground rises rapidly. Follow signs for

Svartifoss. The trails are well marked and obvious but the surface can be uneven with loose gravel, tree roots and small rocky outcrops. At the top of the crest, you will head further inland to a junction of several routes. Once again follow signs for Svartifoss and as you climb, the falls will come into view slightly to the left.

2 Svartifoss

Svartifoss is called 'Black Falls' because the cascade drops over a curtain of perfectly formed black basalt columns. The falls have a fringe of verdant plant life, adding contrast to its dark walls. You can walk down the hill and across the stream to explore behind the cascade but beware of getting wet.
Return along the path you came until you reach a junction of footpaths. Follow arrows signposted Sel. Cross the small bridge and walk up the rise and through a small car park. Follow the road for a few hundred metres until you come to a right junction again marked Sel. Follow the signs and the well-marked path.

3 Sel

The Sel turf and stone farmhouses mark the continuation of occupation in the region since the original settlement. Skaftafell farm was first founded on the plain but it was washed away by *jökulhlaup* and other volcanic activity and the domain was moved uphill. The ruins of the first farmhouse on-site, Gömlutún, can still be explored.
From Sel, follow the footpath through the farmstead and climb to Hæðir.

4 Hæðir

Hæðir means 'high ground'. As you climb through the scrub and brushland, look south as the vast plains of Skeiðarársandur spread out before you. You will begin to see the many glacial creeks that drain to the sea. These change course regularly and are one of the reasons why the *sandur* was all but impassable until modern times.
Return from Hæðir past Sel to the junction and turn right.

5 Bölti

Bölti is the nearest working farm to the national park and offers B&B should you find yourself stuck for accommodation (*Tel: 478 1626*).
Continue down the road until it reaches the valley bottom, then pick up the footpath leading back to the Visitor Centre, crossing the campsite once again.

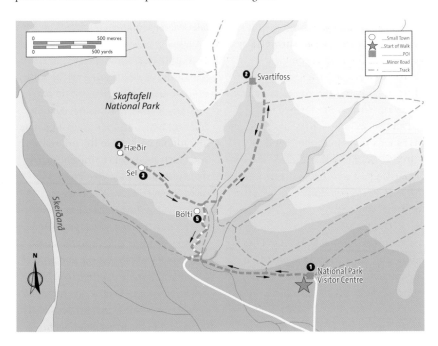

Walk: The Bird Sanctuary at Dyrhólæy

This small outcrop and its surrounding coastline have some of the best birdwatching conditions in the country. Dyrhólæy is a protected site and is off-limits at certain times of the year (e.g. during the nesting period, which lasts through most of May until around 25 June). Carry water and a snack as the nearest cafés and shops are in Vík, 10km (6 miles) east of the site.

Time: 3 hours. Distance: 6km (3¾ miles).

The wedge-shaped headland is reached across a narrow isthmus. Leave your car at the small parking area just before the gate and off you go.

1 Coastal Shallows

As you walk, you will see the ground of Dyrhólæy rising up in front of you (120m/394ft). To your left is a tranquil

Puffins breed in the summer months

stretch of shallow seawater protected by the rock. Here you can spot several species of waders, plus foraging swans and groups of eiders.

Continue to the end of the connecting spit where the road begins to climb. The track can be used by cars as there are car parks on the cliff tops ahead. It is wide enough for several people to walk abreast, so you need not walk on the grass; but the surface can be slippery with loose stones so watch your footing.

After a few hundred metres of climbing, the road splits. Keep to the left and continue to climb. The track swings round with the curve of the cliff leading you to the car park in the southeastern flank. Climb the path to the lookout point.

2 Iron Winches

The remains of several powerful British forged-iron winches indicate old industry. Looking west, you'll get your first glimpse of the rock feature that gives Dyrhólæy its name, 'doorway hill island'.

The huge open arch below was carved out of the rock by the sea.
Turn left and walk for a few metres.

3 Reynisdrangar Needles

There are impressive views east towards Vík, a long black sand spit and the famous Reynisdrangar Needles, offshore basalt stacks, are easily visible on a good day.
From this vantage point, set off walking west, past point 2 and along the well-worn path across the cliff tops.

4 Cliff tops

The sheer black cliffs of Dyrhólæy are ideal breeding sites for seabirds.
Stay on the path and you will eventually reach the lighthouse on the southwestern tip of the cape.

5 Lighthouse

This is the highest spot on Dyrhólæy at 120m (394ft), and the southernmost cliff top in Iceland. From the cliff tops, look east to see the opposing face of the huge arch.
From the lighthouse, follow the track down past the grassland and you will see the shallows to the south come into view once again. The route is steep in parts here, so take care with your footing. Once at the junction, turn left and walk back to your starting point.

For a different perspective of the sanctuary, you can take a trip along the black sand beach and in the sea (weather permitting) in an amphibious vehicle. Tel: 487 8500. www.dyrholaey.com. Admission charge.

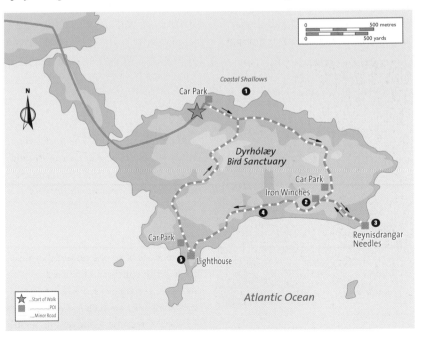

Fishing

It is difficult to overestimate the importance of fishing and fish products to Icelanders both as a provider of employment and economic well-being and as a filler of national coffers. Some say that the sea is in every Icelander's blood, whether as an heir of the legacy of the exploring/invading Vikings or as a farmer of the sea. From its roots as a poor agricultural country at the end of the 1900s, it would be true to say that without fishing, Iceland would not be as wealthy as it is today. Fish and fish products make up 70 per cent of Iceland's export of goods and the industry employs 6 per cent of the workforce.

Icelandic trawler

The island benefits from a shallow continental shelf and the Gulf Stream bringing warm water up from the Caribbean past the eastern coast of the USA and the UK. This shelf is where the nutrients of the cold Arctic waters meet the warm current.

The country is subject to strict fish quotas for economic and ecological reasons, although the Iceland Marine Research Institute sees reasons to be cheerful. Should Iceland join the EU, its exclusive fishing grounds will be under extreme stress. It's a highly sensitive political issue.

Why?

Iceland benefited from the development of salt processing in the early 19th century. This allowed fresh fish to be preserved so that they could reach distant markets. Fish freezing began in the 1930s and expanded rapidly; by 1950 it was a major component of the industry, a situation that continues to this day.

Iceland has embraced the technological revolution in both fish harvesting and fish processing. Fresh fish in market stalls by the harbour is not the Icelandic way as it is in the Mediterranean basin. The plants here are state of the art and the industry

Fisherman unloading

here is the most advanced in the world, incorporating more freezing trawlers – ships that have freezing capability on board – than any other. This means that the fish can be processed and frozen even before they reach Iceland's shores.

Products

Sea fish, shrimp and other shellfish form the bulk of whole-fish products.

The sea fish finds its way around the Mediterranean basin where it forms the staple of dishes such as *bacalao* in Portugal or France. Icelandic salmon, *lax* (salmon treated with black peppers) and salmon fillets tend to be sold in smoked or preserved form.

Dried fish and fish-heads make their way into fish-stock cubes. Fish oils have several uses: cod liver oil for human consumption and marine oils for industry. Fishmeal is a major component of animal feed or of natural fertilisers on farmland.

Major markets

Tonnes of fish are sold at auctions in Iceland's ports in pre-frozen state. Processed later in plants in the destination country, these could go anywhere in the world.

The salted fish, though declining in its share of overall percentage of production, is predominantly shipped to the Mediterranean coast where salted cod has for the last century or so been a traditional foodstuff and the base of many dishes. Iceland's salted cod can be found in fish markets from Portugal through France and Italy to Greece.

Fishmeal from Iceland forms a major component in cattle-feeding programmes worldwide, while its fish oil still plays a role in keeping machinery working smoothly.

Getting away from it all

It is very easy to leave the world behind in Iceland. With a population density of 2.9 people per sq km (1.1 per sq mile) and over a third of the total population living in Reykjavík, you need to travel less than half an hour outside the capital to be all alone. It follows, then, that this is one destination where you don't need to work hard or be addicted to 'extreme' sports to experience the wilderness, though you may still have to take 'roads less travelled', pulling yourself away from route 1, the main ring road.

We would not advise exploring on your own far off the beaten track without a 4WD vehicle, a good map or GPS system, warm clothing, back-up rations and a fully charged mobile phone. We also advise that you tell someone of your travel plans so that in case of emergency an alarm can be raised for you.

If you are unsure of travelling on your own, resort to one of the regular summer tours that take the responsibility for getting you to the places you want to see. These usually cater to small specialist groups, so you will still feel like an intrepid individual rather than a faceless number, particularly if you take a monster-truck 4WD tour.

Hiring a guide is a good idea – you don't need to be a group to do this and it can pay dividends in the quality of the experience you have, especially on the wilder walking and hiking routes.

THE CENTRAL HIGHLANDS

Iceland's central core – known as 'the highlands' – is one of Europe's last great wildernesses. Off-limits to all except those with special vehicles and Arctic experience in winter, it opens its door just a little in summer to let intrepid travellers take a peek. Much of the highlands are in fact featureless plains like the steppes of Mongolia, though remote volcanoes and glaciers add visual interest.

There are two main access points for vehicles travelling from Reykjavík. Each is given a route name and a road number, and each has its own degree of difficulty plus its own attractions. The

The central highlands

routes are not interconnected but the more difficult Sprengisandur Route offers more interconnecting routes at its northern end.

The Kjölur Route

The most accessible is the Kjölur Route or route 35 heading northeast from above Gullfoss and cutting between the Langjökull and Hofsjökull glaciers to hit route 1 east of Blönduós. There is a bus service on this route in summer. The highlights of the trip include Hvaravellir with its geothermal fields renowned for their vivid colours; Hvítárvatn, or the 'white river lake', with its iceberg decoration courtesy of Langjökull; and Kerlingarfjöll with its archetypal 'alpine' scenery.

Kverkfjöll Ice Caves

Another dramatic route runs south from route 1 just east of Moðrudalur. The Kverkfjöll route leads eventually to a compact but fascinating area of natural wonders, the Kverkfjöll Ice Caves. These caverns sit in an area of intense geothermal activity, and the heat and ice interact to create a vast and ever-changing ice sculpture interspersed with plumes of hot escaping steam.

The Sprengisandur Route

This route (F26) is famed for its vast sand deserts, monotonous to some but surreally inspiring to others. The route rises from the northern flank of Hekla (*see p121*) and travels between

Getting away from it all

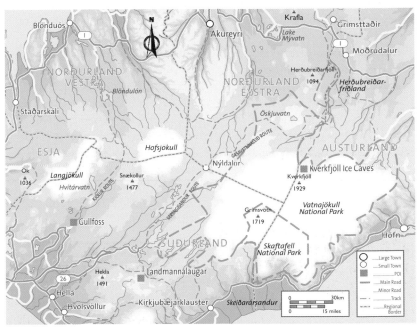

Hofsjökull and Vatnajökull National Park (*see pp126–8*) into the hinterland. It is taxing for vehicles and requires patience but once past the Nýldalur mountain hut it branches out offering several choices to the central northern coast and eastern Iceland.

The easternmost route of these choices, the Gæsavatnnaleið Route, takes you to the spectacular Askja Caldera, with an interior area of 50sq km (19sq miles), and the dark lake Öskjuvatn. The caldera was created in 1875 from a massive eruption that brought dark days to much of Europe. You will also be able to visit Herðubreið, a subglacial volcano that has somehow lost its snowy cap, and the surrounding foreboding lava fields.

Dettifoss at the Jökulsárgljúfur National Park

THE FAR NORTHEAST

Iceland's far northeastern corner does not have the dramatic natural attractions of the central highlands. However, it is one of the least populated and least visited parts of Iceland.

You can access the route north out of the Jökulsárgljúfur National Park (*see opposite*), where route 85 leads east around Melrakkaslétta into Þistilfjörður and then around on to the Langanes Peninsula before skirting Bakkaflói and heading south to Vopnafjörður (*see p115*).

Melrakkaslétta is the nearest point on mainland Iceland to the midnight sun and Raufarhöfn is its northernmost village. Its coastline is mostly low lying,

with numerous small inland lakes and coastal reefs, plus the spectacular **Rauðinúpur** ('Red cliffs'), so called because the layers of iron oxide in the rocks are a vivid red. It is Iceland's newest bird trail, with all the black birds of Iceland together (guillemots, auks and puffins) plus gyr falcons and ptarmigans.

At Langanes, the road runs out two-thirds of the way along the peninsula, so a 4WD vehicle is advised, if only for comfort. The once-rich farmlands here have mostly been abandoned, and numerous buildings stand sentinel in the fields. The end of the peninsula is

AND THEN THERE WERE TWO

Legend has it that catastrophe struck northern Melrakkaslétta when the plague wiped out the whole population except for one woman in the east and one man in the west. They met up at Meyjarþúfa (Virgin's Knoll), west of Raufarhöfn, and became mother and father to a whole new generation that repopulated the area.

marked by yet another lighthouse, built in 1910.

Please refer to the map on p91 for this area.

JÖKULSÁRGLJÚFUR NATIONAL PARK

Already mentioned in the northern Iceland section, Jökulsárgljúfur merits inclusion here because only a few of its many visitors venture away from Dettifoss, its major attraction and the 'Grand Canyon'-type panoramas from the major viewing points. There are also interesting short day routes: through the abandoned gorge exit at Asbyrgi in the north (1-hour round trip from the car park); to Hólmatungur (a 4-hour hike from Dettifoss or by a 4WD vehicle) with its wonderful meadowland and waterfalls; to Hljóðaklettar, or 'Echoing Rocks' (1-hour round trip from the car park), where the sound of the river is diverted through the gullies between the eroded basalt boulders; and to nearby Rauðhólar (2-hour round trip from the car park), a series of small red volcanic craters.

The *pièce de résistance* is the two-day hike along the gorge rim from the base of Dettifoss to the mouth of the gorge at Asbyrgi. This route takes in many of the highlights above in addition to the aforementioned falls, and there is camping en route. It is a popular trail so you won't be too far from human company – unlike the Strandir routes (*see below*).

THE WESTFJORDS REGION

Please refer to the map on p77 for this area.

Strandir

A world away from Iceland's 'fire and ice' image, Strandir is still one of the country's most magnificent regions. A rocky peninsula forming the northernmost section of the Westfjords,

Getting away from it all

Hafragilsundirlendi, valley of Jökulsá á Fjöllum at the Jökulsárgljúfur National Park

An abandoned farmhouse in the Adalvik cove at Hornstrandir

it is scarcely populated. Designated the Hornstrandir Nature Reserve and protected in the south by mighty Drangajökull, the park has no roads – just 500sq km (193sq miles) of upland heath and tundra to explore.

Access is by boat from Ísafjörður (*see pp82–4*) or Holmavík (*see p81*) to several small coves with basic accommodation (it is essential to book these ahead of time) and eateries, or on foot from the tiny towns on its southwesterly and southeasterly flanks. You can use the boats like water taxis to drop you off at several bays over a number of days, taking short hikes and returning to the same starting point. Or you can link several trails to turn a day or overnight expedition into one lasting several days. Remote abandoned homesteads, mewing birds, deserted hot

springs and no sound but that of your own thoughts are some of the delights here. The Strandir is also one of the last refuges of the Arctic fox in Iceland and you may be lucky enough to see one on your trip.

A popular and relatively easy route is to take the boat from Ísafjörður to Sæból and then walk across Strandir Peninsula to Hesteyri, where you will be picked up by boat the following day. Although this barely scratches the surface of what Strandir affords, it still offers some exceptional scenery.

Don't forget that for longer inland hikes you will need equipment, water and food – a night under the stars will be one of your most memorable ones on the island. If you would rather have things organised for you, several organisations run guided tours.

See the Sport and leisure section (pp160–65).

The western Westfjords

The westernmost fjords of the Westfjords offer landscapes similar to Strandir with a few more creature comforts. Here it is possible to link short hikes with car journeys and to spend your nights in a comfortable bed.

The further west you travel, the more remote you get. Farmsteads drop in number, and vehicles, too. At the head of every fjord are towering cliffs – some of Iceland's finest bird-breeding locations – and the roads sweep from the waterside up and over the high plateaux in a series of breathtaking passes. This is the most westerly land in Europe and standing on the cliffs or at the water's edge you really feel a sense of wonder looking west towards Greenland.

FROM DISTANT SHORES

The island of Æðey just south of Strandir, the largest island in Ísafjörðardjúp, is now a nesting ground for eider ducks. In 1615, a Spanish boat was shipwrecked there and the sailors settled on the island. Local legend has it that they became aggressive towards the locals, and local chieftain, Ari Magnússon, organised a posse, hunted them down and killed them all.

Getting away from it all

Take a trip on a whale-watching boat

Mountains tower behind an isolated cottage

Látrabjarg Peninsula

The highlight of the southern peninsula are the cliffs around Látrabjarg in the southwestern corner: over 10km (6 miles) of towering rock reaching 400m (1,312ft) in height that is prime seabird nesting territory with all the major species found in one place. The locals have made a business out of collecting eggs and chicks by scaling the cliff face by rope – not a task for the faint-hearted.

To reach the cliffs involves a long drive across Látraheiði where you will need to leave the car and set out on foot for the last few kilometres to reach the breeding grounds and magnificent views. At Hvallátur, on the same peninsula, is the westernmost home in Europe. East across the moors is Hnjótur, where you will find the little-visited **Folk Museum at Hnjótur**. This unique museum includes artefacts used by people living in the area over the last few generations, plus, rather surprisingly, an aviation museum.

HELP!

In 1947, the trawler *Dhoon* was shipwrecked off Látrabjarg and a dangerous rescue mission was mounted from Hvallátur with Icelanders scaling down the cliffs to pick up the exhausted seamen. When a film crew came to document the event they found another trawler in trouble in the same spot and managed to film the second rescue minute by minute.

The beaches on this peninsula are considered to be the best in Iceland, backed by cliffs or long spits protecting the coastal shallows.
Folk Museum: tel: 456 1511. www.hnjotur.is. Open: daily end May–mid-Sept 10am–6pm, but if closed call the museum manager on 456 1569, who can open it on request. Admission charge.

The Þingeyri region
Like stubby fingers, the outcrops around Þingeyri point northwestward towards Greenland. Route 60 cuts across the knuckles of this hand, taking most visitors with it fast-tracking into Ísafjörður through the road tunnel, but the peninsulas here have some incredibly wild upland to explore including vast scree slopes.

Few roads cut into the heart of this region but the 624 leading from Mýrar on the north coast of Dýrarfjörður past Thverfell to Sæból makes a splendid if rough journey – on a clear day the views are majestic.

Getting away from it all

The cliffs of Látrabjarg

Spas and well-being

The lifespan of an average Icelander (81 years for men and 86 for women) is among the highest in the world. While many put this down to a shot of cod liver oil with breakfast (you, too, can partake of this during your stay as they usually have bottles of the oil at your breakfast buffet – complete with its fishy taste and smell), there is no doubt that the thermal waters have a lot to do with their good health.

Long before geothermal technology, Icelanders used the hot water generated by the country's

Geothermal steam rises from the Blue Lagoon

volcanoes for everyday well-being – after all, it was right on the doorstep and a great benefit in the cold winter weather. Hotpots and natural hot springs were regularly used to warm cold bodies and over time they became meeting and socialising places – like the Brits developed the pub, Icelanders developed the hot spring. All communities, no matter how scattered, will have a community hotpot and pool, and this is really the best way to break the ice – excuse the pun – with the locals.

Large hotpots, such as Laugar Spa in Reykjavík (see p43), consist of several small circular pools of differing temperatures. To get the maximum benefit, it is sensible to spend several minutes in each of the pools, moving from the coolest to the warmest, before plunging into a temperate zone. This helps to liven blood circulation, promote muscle tone and keep the heart healthy. Community pots may have only one pool of constant heat but there is always a swimming pool close by for the contrast in temperature.

There are two major geothermal centres in Iceland. First, the Blue Lagoon, which is probably the country's most famous attraction; you

The spa at Lake Mývatn

can visit by bus directly from the airport so that you can begin the process of relaxing as soon as you arrive. The waters of the Blue Lagoon are full of beneficial elements including natural minerals to aid healthy skin, and remedy a whole list of ailments from arthritis to psoriasis. The beneficial properties have also been packaged in a range of skin and haircare products that you can take home with you. Another option is the spa centre at Lake Mývatn, which takes advantage of the geothermal heat just beneath its surface, and is in a real beauty spot.

Many pools also have saunas and steam rooms. Here swimwear is normally abandoned for bare skin,

whatever your age – this is part of the relaxation process. A strategically placed towel is standard as you enter or leave. In natural pools in the highlands, such as Landmannalaugar, bathing clothes are optional.

You can spend time in the spa before your day starts – many communal pools open early – or to relax after a day's sightseeing. You will soon begin to feel the change: skin that is smooth and clear, and a body that feels more relaxed. Enjoy!

ETIQUETTE

Icelanders don't use hotpots to get clean. It is mandatory to wash thoroughly with soap and water before entering a communal hotpot or pool area.

Shopping

Iceland offers some interesting and unusual souvenirs over and above the run-of-the-mill T-shirt or fridge magnet – though there is no shortage of kitsch cuddly puffins or models of whales in snowdomes. Well-designed and artisan-produced souvenirs form a large sector of the market, though prices are higher for these quality objects. Reykjavík's main shopping street, Laugavegur, is known for its cutting-edge fashion, jewellery and art.

WHAT TO BUY
Art

If Icelanders are not making music, they tend to be making art – though more than a few can do both. The national psyche tends towards modernism rather than realism. There are always several gallery exhibitions in progress whatever time of year you visit, so make time to discover a new cutting-edge artist to add to your collection. Glass and ceramics are also favourite media with Iceland's artists.

Antiques on sale in Reykjavik

You will also find a range of excellent souvenir photograph collections to grace your coffee table and to recall your trip.

Beauty products

The Blue Lagoon markets a range of facial and skincare products enhanced with the minerals found in the thermal pools that you can carry when you return home. There is a shop at the lagoon itself, at Laugavegur 15 in Reykjavík, and in the airport departure lounge.

Clothing

There are some interesting options in clothing. The wool of Icelandic sheep has been used for centuries to produce warm lopapeysa sweaters with traditional patterns and designs which can form the signature souvenir of your trip – and, of course, is a very practical item for use during your stay. The very best are still hand-knitted but these are also correspondingly expensive.

If you prefer practical clothing but more contemporary in style, a couple of companies make ideal garments for an outdoor lifestyle and for the unpredictable weather of the country. Try 66° North, Alafoss or Cintamani. Reykjavík plays host to some exceptional fashion designers, so if you want to wear something that isn't off the high street but has a great deal of style, try shopping at Verksmidjan, ELM or Kraum along Laugavegur.

Lopapeysa sweaters in a Reykjavík shop

Jewellery

There are excellent jewellery designers across the island but most are found in the design district of Reykjavík (*see below*). For modern, one-of-a-kind pieces, it would be difficult to beat the choice here. Look for items using lavastone – a rock that is obviously very pertinent to the area – or reproductions of runic symbols and Viking designs.

Natural products

Wool is one of the high-quality natural products found in Iceland. Others include horn, bone, stone and lavastone, which are turned into beautiful objects or carved into modern sculpture.

WHERE TO SHOP
Reykjavík

For that unique design product, walk the length of Laugavegur, the main shopping street, and Skólavörðustígur – an area known as the design district, where the shops are filled with crafts, jewellers and small clothing boutiques.

There are also two large American-style shopping malls filled with individual boutiques and more recognisable international brands. Both Kringlan and Smáralind are great places to shop, especially when the weather isn't behaving, although shops are largely international.

If you wish to bargain hunt, visit the atmospheric flea market where all Reykjavíkians, from the trendiest to the most bohemian, head each weekend. Kolaportið, set in an old warehouse next to the Hafnarhús, sells second-hand clothing, china and collectibles, as well as cheap DVDs and CDs – though it is difficult to ensure the quality or authenticity of the recordings.

12 Tónar

The place to buy Icelandic music and sometimes catch a live concert. There is always a complimentary espresso while you listen, with no purchase necessary. *Skólavörðustígur 15. Tel: 511 5656. www.12tonar.is*

66° North

Taking its name from the latitude of the Arctic Circle, this outdoor-pursuits shop is synonymous with adventure sports in Iceland and the place to come for seriously warm long-lasting clothes. *Bankastræti 5. Tel: 517 6020. www.66north.com*

Aurum

Guðbjörg Kristin Ingvarsdóttir, the designer behind this contemporary jewellery shop, has won many awards for her stunning designs, inspired by Icelandic nature. The precious metals and shapes have a refreshingly modern take but still look timeless. *Bankastræti 4. Tel: 551 2770. www.aurum.is*

Eggert the Furrier

This master furrier with an international clientele has a distinctive collection of furs, leathers, fish-skins and cashmere scarves. *Skólavörðustígur 38. Tel: 551 1121. www.furrier.is*

TAX REFUND

If you spend more than ISK 4,000 in a tax-free, accredited shop during your stay, and keep your receipts, you are entitled to a tax refund, provided the goods leave Iceland within three months of purchase.

Make sure that you get a Global Refund Cheque with your sales receipt, and that this is signed by the sales assistant.

If you are leaving via Keflavík airport, and you are claiming back less than ISK 5,000, all you need to do is to take the Global Refund Cheques to the Landsbanki desk in the transit hall on the upper floor, and you will receive a cash refund. There is also a kiosk in the same building as the Reykjavík Tourist Office. Alternatively, post your completed Global Refund Cheques and receive a refund on your credit card after about five weeks.

ELM

This minimal shop specialises in 'clothing designed by women for women', primarily inspired by the Icelandic landscape. *Laugavegur 1. Tel: 511 0991. www.elm.is*

The Blue Lagoon shop in Reykjavík sells all kinds of skincare products

Gullkúnst Helgu

Handmade gold and silver jewellery with lavastone, precious and semi-precious gems and stones.
Laugavegur 13. Tel: 561 6660.
www.gullkunst.is

Kirsuberjatréð

Design gallery run by 11 female designers producing a variety of conversation pieces for the home, from local fortune-telling games to fish-skin belts to woollen and felt items.
Vesturgata 4. Tel: 562 8990. www.kirs.is

Kraum Icelandic Design

This interior design and art shop is situated in a renovated wooden building dating back to 1752. It offers exhibition space, as well as multiple levels to showcase the range of original clothing, accessories and objects they sell.
Aðalstræti 10. Tel: 517 7797.
www.kraum.is

Steinnun

High fashion taking inspiration from Iceland's wilderness. Expect minimalist chic with the odd unexpected ruffle, piece of fur or tulle. Steinnun herself has had international success and was voted Iceland's Artist of the Year in 2009.
Bankastræti 9. Tel: 588 8849.
www.steinnun.com

Outside of Reykjavík
Alafoss

A factory outlet store north of Reykjavík with a range of knitwear, plus a craft centre and art gallery for one-of-a-kind items.
Álafossvegur 23, 270 Mosfellsbær.
Tel: 566 6303. www.alafoss.is.
Also at Laugavegur 1, Reykjavík.

Hafþór Ragnar Þórhallsson

Exquisite artisan bird carvings that can only be bought here – well worth the trip to the middle of nowhere. Next door to the Museum of Icelandic Sorcery and Witchcraft.
Höfðagata 12, Holmavík. Tel: 451 3162.
www.northwest.is

HR Chocolates

This small experimental bakery in Mosfellsbær and Reykjavík has been lauded as one of the top 100 chocolatiers in the world. Chocolates include real fruit, chilli and ginger.
Háholt 13–15, Mosfellsbær and Háaleitisbraut 58–60, Reykjavík.

Skaftafell Cultural Centre

This centre in a renovated Norse house (1907) has a resident population of artists throughout the summer and holds numerous exhibitions. Works are for sale.
Austurvegur 42, Seyðisfjörður.
Tel: 472 1632.

Skógar Museum Shop

This shop in the Skógar Museum has a good range of books, arts, woollen goods and handmade jewellery.
Skógar Museum, 861 Hvolsvöllur.
Tel: 487 8845. www.skogarsafn.is

Entertainment

The backbone of the daytime social scene is the coffee house. In a country that does not have a tradition of drinking alcohol (beer was illegal until 1989 and alcohol is expensively taxed), coffee is the drink of choice. It is served in copious amounts – refills are almost always free – and is freshly ground.

REYKJAVÍK
Coffee house culture

Coffee houses are places for people to meet and chat. There are always newspapers and magazines lying around, and some double up as galleries for art exhibitions. Some coffee houses also serve alcohol, blurring the boundaries between a café and bar. But a relaxed atmosphere is true of every one. They are great places to feel the pulse of the city. Smoking is banned in public places.

Café Cultura

Low-key welcoming café inside the Intercultural Centre with a well-priced international menu, particularly good for students or those on a budget.
Hverfisgata 18. Tel: 530 9314.

Café Paris

This popular city centre meeting place is more famed for its summer terrace, where locals come to see and be seen, rather than for its food.
Austurstræti 14. Tel: 551 1020.

Grái Kötturinn

The 1950s-style basement café 'Grey Cat' is a favourite brunch spot for locals, serving up American-inspired pancakes with maple syrup and bacon, and Illy coffee. Unusual art on the walls, too.
Hverfisgata 16a. Tel: 551 1544.

Mokka Kaffi

An original Reykjavík coffee house, Mokka Kaffi opened in 1958 and brought in the island's first espresso machine. Mokka Kaffi is also famous for its hot chocolate and waffles. There are regular art exhibitions where you can buy the works on display.
Skólavörðustígur 3a. Tel: 552 1174.

Nightlife

Pre-economic crash, Reykjavík's nightlife put it literally on top of the world, with superstar DJs and low-fi bands entertaining clubbers and drinkers from far and wide. These days it's still a buzzing place on a Friday and

THE *RUNTUR*

The Saturday night pub crawl in Reykjavík is so legendary it has its own name. Locals move from bar to bar and consume vast amounts of alcohol in a short space of time, so things can sometimes get a little silly and noisy – but generally people remain well behaved.

Saturday night, but its nightlife has definitely peaked.

Don't start too early – particularly in summer – as the party will go on all night long until the following morning. Most drinkers don't hit the bars until midnight, preferring to drink at home beforehand (largely because the alcohol prices are so high). Keep it cheaper by drinking non-imported beer and don't miss the local firewater, aniseedy Brennivín, drunk in shots like tequila.

101 Bar

The upmarket bar of design hotel 101 serves cocktails, wine and spirits to ambient music. Stylish staff and slightly older clientele than in the bars in town. *101 Hotel, Hverfisgata 10. Tel: 580 0101. www.101hotel.is*

Grand Rokk

This two-level bar has a space downstairs where you can play chess or simply chat. Upstairs, live rock'n'roll is offered most nights and the bar offers a great selection of malt whiskies. *Smiðjustigur 6. Tel: 551 5522.*

Kaffibarinn

Reykjavík's most famous bar, all shabby chic sofas and retro chandeliers, is transformed with DJs and dancing into the small hours at weekends, while

Sólon café/bar and bistro, Reykjavík

New Year's Night, Reykjavík

open for coffee during the day. Expect queues out of the door.
Bergstaðastræti 1. Tel: 551 1588.

Kaffi Reykjavík

A little bit of everything, this place pulls people in for its buffet dinner, drinks and live music and dancing. Try the Ice Bar for a really chilling experience, where you will be given a coat to help you with the -6°C (21°F) temperature, plus cocktails and Brennivín.
Vesturgata 2. Tel: 552 3030.
www.kaffireykjavík.is

Prikið

Reykjavík's oldest bar serves coffee during the day and a scrum of arty types with beer in the evenings. A little bit of an old-man pub at times, it's still got a real charm to it. Live music on Fridays.
Bankastræti 12. www.prikid.is

Vínbarinn

The only dedicated wine bar in Iceland with a good range of reds and whites from around the world.
Kirkjutorg 3. Tel: 552 4120.

Clubs

Boston

Hard to find but worth it when you get there, this bar/club on the top floor above a shop is grungy and indie in the old-school way. A real hit with the locals, with some really quirky design features such as stuffed animals and heavy velvet curtains.
Laugavegur 28b. Tel: 517 7816.

Kaffi Sólon

This stylish bar has a cool clientele and great DJs, and Sólon is also a great café/bar and bistro during the week. The upper floor is a busy nightclub at weekends.
Bankastræti 7a. Tel: 562 3232.

REYKJAVÍK DANCE FESTIVAL

The annual Reykjavík Dance Festival brings international troupes and choreographers to the island each September. The diverse programme includes a parade and various indoor and outdoor settings. Tickets and information at Borgarleikhúsið. *Tel: 862 6023.*
www.dancefestival.is

NASA

This former theatre is known for its good acoustics as well as the live concerts that it hosts from time to time. It's the biggest club in the centre of the city.
Austurvöllur Square.
Tel: 511 1313.

Vegamót

This cool, funky neon-lit venue is another combination of bistro/bar/ café and club. The clientele is young, chic and beautiful.
Vegamótastigur. Tel: 511 3040.
www.vegamot.is

The arts

With the emphasis on partying, one might be forgiven for thinking that the arts play little part in today's entertainment, but nothing could be further from the truth.

In 2012, the opening of the Tónlistarhús (the Icelandic National Concert & Conference Centre and Hotel) by the harbour will be a major cultural coup for the city and Iceland's expanding musical scene. The futuristic outer shell of the building was designed by the prominent artist Ólafur Elíasson – this will create a connection between the building and its surroundings, such as the spectacular water plaza Reykjatorg, a work of art in itself. The internal concert halls and the rest of the complex were designed by Henning Larsen Tegnestue, a topflight architectural firm from Copenhagen.

FINGER ON THE PULSE

For an up-to-date and somewhat irreverent view of what's happening in Iceland today, the English-language *Grapevine Magazine* is available free in cafés, galleries and tourist offices. Its publishers also run the annual Airwaves Festival. *Iceland Review* is the very best magazine to pick up if you're interested in culture and lifestyle around the country. Available in bookshops, it's also blessed with the images of award-winning photographer and deputy editor Páll Stefánsson.

Borgarleikhúsið (City Theatre)

Home of the arts in the capital, the huge stage of the Borgarleikhúsið is complemented by an intimate studio workspace. The theatre hosts a wide range of performances from avant-garde theatre to political debates. It is home to two companies, Reykjavík City Theatre, a 24-strong professional company offering at least six productions each year, and the Icelandic Dance Company.
Listabraut 3. Tel: 568 5500.
www.borgarleikhusid.is

Icelandic Opera

The Icelandic Opera has a short and very popular season each year. For the rest of the year the venue plays host to a range of visiting domestic and international repertory theatre companies with plenty of performances in English.
Ingólfsstræti. Tel: 511 4200. www.opera.is

Icelandic Symphony Orchestra

The professional company hosts a full and varied programme covering classical

The Culture House in Reykjavík

compositions and modern pieces. It usually performs in the Háskólabíó (University Cinema Auditorium). *Háskólabíð v/Hagatorg. Tel: 545 5200. www.sinfonia.is*

Salurinn Concert Hall
Iceland's most technologically advanced performance venue with a programme from Vivaldi to Cole Porter. *Hamraborg 4–6, Kópavogur. Tel: 570 0400. www.salurinn.is*

BEYOND REYKJAVÍK
For a small and widely scattered population, the rest of Iceland still has a vibrant artistic scene. Two hotspots are Akureyri in the north and Seyðisfjörður in the east.

From the middle of June until early August, the Cultural Centre in Akureyri (*Listagil. Tel: 466 2609. www.listagilakureyri.is*) runs exhibitions and concerts in its annual Festival of the Arts. Performances run the gamut of visual art, music, theatre and literature. In winter, the Akureyri Drama Society (*Hafnarstræti 57. Tel: 460 0200. www.leikfelag.is*), Iceland's second professional company, stages four or five plays, to keep everyone entertained through the long and dark evenings.

Seyðisfjörður is the cultural centre of the Eastfjords and home to a concentrated population of Icelandic and foreign musicians and artists. Many artists from Reykjavík spend the summer here and the Skaftafell Cultural Centre (*Austurvegur 42. Tel: 472 1632*) is where they hang out, holding exhibitions and animated debates. The Á seyði art festival at Seyðisfjörður takes place at venues around the town between May and September.

AN EVENING WITH THE VIKINGS

The traditionally designed Viking Village at Hafnarfjörður offers the closest thing to a genuine Viking evening with a meal of Norse dishes served by staff in native dress plus some good old pagan singing and *Saga* telling.

The Viking Village hosts a Viking festival every year in June where 21st-century Norsemen gather to celebrate the old ways, or stay in the Viking Rooms of the Viking Hotel. *Strandgata 55, Hafnarfjörður. Tel: 565 1213. www.vikingvillage.is*

Celebrating Culture Night in Reykjavík

Cinema

Cinemas scattered around the island feed the demand for Hollywood all-star films; these are shown in English with Icelandic subtitles. There are several film festivals throughout the year featuring art-house and award-winning foreign-language films, in addition to the highly regarded domestic products. One venue for these is the Háskólabíó (*see the Symphony Orchestra pp155–6*).

Regnboginn is a local city centre cinema at Hverfisgata 54 (*Tel: 551 9000*).

Smárabíó (*Smáralind Shopping Centre. Tel: 564 0000. Bus: 24, 28*) is the largest multiplex in Iceland. Sambíó (*Kringlan Shopping Centre. Tel: 575 8900. www.sambio.is*) is another multiscreen complex.

One thing to remember is that most Icelandic cinemas still have an intermission. This used to be because the film reels needed to be changed or for smokers to have a quick cigarette. Nowadays it's just to sell snacks and drinks.

REYKJAVÍK CULTURE NIGHT

Held every year on the third weekend in August, Reykjavík Culture Night is the biggest such festival in the year with a marathon, exhibitions, street parades, open-air theatre and fireworks displays. All the major museums, galleries, shops and churches are open late and there are events such as re-enactment of a pagan wake, Race of the Waiters (complete with tray and open bottle of wine), live accordion recitals and musical chess. The streets are packed!

Children

Iceland is the kind of place you would love to bring up kids. There is little concern about security and it has been rated as one of the best places in the world to be a mother by the charity Save the Children. Though there are few specific attractions for children, there is plenty to keep them occupied, with zoos, museums and activities to suit both in Reykjavík and beyond.

Animal magic
Free Willy?
The high success rate of whale-watching trips make it a sure-fire way of enthralling children of all ages. Birdwatching trips to islands like Flatey or Grímsey will thrill budding ornithologists, and spotting birds from land can also be rewarding, though some remote cliff sites mean a long walk – the southern Snæfellsnes Peninsula and the cliffs around Vík are easily reached breeding sites for puffins, Arctic terns and many other breeds.

Horse riding
The Icelandic horse is an ideal size for youngsters. It has adult horse sense in its diminutive body, so is not overwhelming for beginners or nervous riders. There is an excellent network of riding centres and stables all across the island, and kids can take instruction or head out on a guided trek on routes that suit the rider's ability. This is a great way to meet other children and make new friends.

The Zoo in Reykjavík
It is more of a petting farm and educational centre, but for most under-10s there is certainly a morning's worth of entertainment here. Lambs, kids and piglets are born every year, so the livestock is entertaining – the same goes for cygnets and ducklings. There are feeding and petting sessions throughout the day, plus a playground with slides and climbing frames.

Natural delights
Children are fascinated by the geothermic activity that is ever-present around the island. Strokker geyser is the most famous and reliable, so that is a must-see, but the stinky steam plumes, hot springs and bubbling mud pools are equally fascinating, especially to older children. Keep small fingers out of hot pools even if silly adults in the vicinity may not be setting a good example.

Sport and leisure
Organised activities

Older children who like activity will have a great time in Iceland. There are many exhilarating outdoor pursuits to sample and enjoy and the professional attitude of the support staff makes Iceland one of the safest places to have a go at something just a little bit daring, including kayaking, quad biking, horse riding and on-and-off-road cycling.

The walking and hiking here is fantastic and there are routes for all levels of fitness.

Swimming pools

Almost every settlement has a communal pool that is usually heated, so they are comfortable throughout the year. For water babies, this is a dream come true, and another great place to make friends with Icelandic children who are introduced to the pools in their first few months. The most famous natural pool, the Blue Lagoon, makes children very welcome.

BE AWARE

Although temperatures may not rise very high in Iceland, the sun is still strong. So it is important to make sure you keep children well topped up with a high-factor sunblock.

Enjoying a ride on an Icelandic horse through the streets of Reykjavík

Sport and leisure

A trip to Iceland is as much about 'what to do' as 'what to see'. The phrase 'the great outdoors' could have been coined specifically for this island where the geography seems to have been designed to cater to the needs of the active sports person. Even if you don't normally enjoy physical activity, the landscapes are so beguiling that they invite you to join them and your outdoor pursuits can be as gentle as you like.

Angling

You will find some of the richest salmon rivers fed by glacial meltwaters here but Iceland has many freshwater species as well. The salmon season runs from 20 June to mid-September, while the trout season is longer, starting in late April. Fishing licences can be expensive but the rivers are carefully managed so a quality experience is assured. For something a little different, try ice-fishing in the depths of winter.

Icelandic Fly Fishing Service (*Storholt 16, 603 Akureyri. Tel: 461 2456. www.tiffs.is*) holds the rights to several northern trout rivers, and has access to salmon and char sites. Be aware that fishing regulations are serious and you will be fined for contravening them.

ATV tours

For a little more speed and adrenalin, try heading out into the wilderness in an all-terrain vehicle. Once you have got to grips with the controls, you can don your helmet and go into the great outdoors following trails and traversing streams, accompanied by an experienced back-up team.

In summer, take control of a 4WD bike, and in winter get behind the handlebars of a snowmobile. ATV Iceland (*www.atviceland.com*) offers tours running from Reykjavík; contact the tourist office for other organisations.

Cyclists touring the fjords

Birdwatching (*see pp168–9*)

Cycling

Iceland offers good cycling trails for beginners, and challenging routes for the fit and experienced. Reykjavík harbour has a cycle path and the fjord floors around the East and West fjords offer easy and picturesque possibilities, though locals might look at you askance. Cycling trips taking in the full island have become popular.

The Icelandic Mountain Bike Club offers a wealth of information (*Brekkhustigur 2, 101 Reykjavík. Tel: 562 0099. www.fjallahjolaklubburinn.is. Clubhouse open: Thur from 8pm*). Iceland Travel Ltd (*Skútuvogur 13a. Tel: 585 4300. www.icelandtravel.is*) offers guided cycle tours around the capital. Guided bike tours of Reykjavík are also available from Iceland Bike (*Tel: 694 8956. www.icelandbike.com*).

Glacier tours and snowmobiling

Heading out on to a glacier is a must-do activity and you can either do this in the relative comfort of a specially modified Arctic truck or drive yourself on a snowmobile as part of a safari tour to feel the real power of raw nature. Dress warm. Glacier Jeeps (*781 Vagnsstaðir. Tel: 478 1000. www.glacierjeeps.is*) runs safaris on Vatnajökull throughout the year.

Golf

Golf is a growing sport in Iceland and most small towns have set 9- or 18-hole courses. In the summer, you can play almost 24 hours a day. The Arctic Open tournament is held on the course at Akureyri on midsummer night with the players teeing off at midnight. Heimæy, in the Westman Islands, is home to a unique golf club

During the summer, golf can be played nearly 24 hours a day

nestled under an extinct volcano, which hosts the Volcano Open Golf Championship every year.
Visit *www.golf.is* for more information.

Hiking

Walking and hiking is perhaps the major pastime for visitors and locals alike. You don't need to be especially fit to enjoy some of Iceland's most impressive landscapes, but comfortable, strong shoes and warm, waterproof clothing are essential.

The national parks at Þingvellir and Skaftafell are perfect places to start, with easy and well-signposted routes. The birdwatching cliffs of the southern Snæfellsnes Peninsula have flat routes running by dramatic seascapes. Every area has walking routes that you can enjoy. Simply head to the tourist office for route maps or buy the more detailed Landmælinger Íslands maps (1:100,000 scale) from bookshops or the city Tourist Office in Reykjavík.

For more serious hikers, Iceland offers some very demanding routes.

The trail along the base of the Jökulsárgljúfur canyon in the north is one. If you intend to take a long or remote route, leave a note with your plans and timescale at your hotel. You will need food supplies and high-quality safety equipment to minimise the risk. There are around 70 mountain cabins that offer basic accommodation for 6 to over 80 people (*see p126 for information on the iconic four-day Laugarvegurinn walk*).

Icelandic Touring Association (*Mörkin 6, 108 Reykjavík. Tel: 568 2533. www.fi.is*) and Icelandic Mountain Guides (*Vagnhöfði 7b, 110 Reykjavík. Tel: 587 9999. www.mountainguide.is*) offer guided walks ranging from easy to difficult, including glacier hikes, and can tailor-make trips for small groups.

Horse riding

Viewing the countryside on horseback is one of the best ways to enjoy Iceland, and you will find stables all around the country. You will need a little instruction to master the technique required for the

Hiking is one of Iceland's most popular pastimes

Trotting along on horseback is a great way to view the countryside

shorter Icelandic horses (*see pp166–7*) even if you are already experienced, but once you have gained the confidence there are numerous bridle paths to explore. You can simply hire a horse for a couple of hours to take a short guided trip, or take a day tour with lunch included, or decide to enjoy the whole of your holiday on horseback on long-distance treks.

Located in Hveragerði, Eldhestar Stables and Countryside Hotel runs short and long treks riding tours from its base, past scenic farmhouses and through rivers, around the Blue Lagoon, Gullfoss and Geysir with pick-ups from Reykjavík hotels all year round (*810 Hveragerði. Tel: 480 4800. www.eldhestar.is*).

Please note: in recent years some stables have been reported to have taken on overly large groups of inexperienced riders who are not regularly monitored for loose saddles and other safety issues. Check on the stable's reputation with the local tourist office before riding, which is at your own risk, and express any concern to the guides, who may then keep a closer eye on you.

Jeep safaris

The jeep is the perfect way to enjoy the excitement of the Icelandic countryside. These chunky vehicles with their huge tyres are perfectly designed for the challenging terrain. Most tours last a full day, but you can also take longer jeep treks.

Mountaineers of Iceland (*Skútuvogur 12, Reykjavík. Tel: 580 9900. www.mountaineers.is*) offers tours of the southwestern part of Iceland from

Seeing the countryside by quad bike is unforgettable

the capital and Highland Expedition Tours, Fjallasyn (*Smiðjusteigur 7, Reykjahverfi, 641 Húsavík. Tel: 464 3940. www.fjallasyn.is*) runs tours to Lake Mývatn and the Jökulsárgljúfur region from the north.

Kayaking

The sheltered waters of the fjords are dramatic places to try sea kayaking for the first time, while the lakes and lower reaches of the rivers offer perfect inland conditions. From a kayak you can get a bird's-eye view of the migrating and native gulls, explore coastal caves and inlets, or stop on the riverbank miles away from anywhere to enjoy a rudimentary picnic in the silence.

In the capital, Ultima Thule Expeditions (*Bíldshöfði 16. Tel: 567 8978. www.ute.is*) runs guided tours. Arctic Adventures (*Laugavegur 11, Reykjavík. Tel: 562 7000. www.adventures.is*) also runs a variety of sea-kayaking tours from Reykjavík and Ísafjörður in fjords, lakes and

the North Atlantic. It can also tailor-make tours.

Skiing

Though by no means as challenging or well developed as the European Alps or the North American Rockies, Iceland has a number of small ski stations. Because of the long winter days, the runs tend to be illuminated, adding an extra touch of fun to the experience. Don't expect après-ski.

Close to the capital, the Bláfjöll ski centre (*Tel: 530 3000. http://skidasvaedi.is*) has 11 lifts with runs up to 10km (6 miles) in length and there are daily buses from Reykjavík when the runs are open. You can hire equipment and get instruction here. There are other multiple-run centres at Akureyri, Dalvík, Eskifjörður, Hengilssæði, Ísafjörður, Sigulfjörður and Skálafell.

Whale-watching

Húsavík styles itself the 'Whale-Watching Capital of the World' and it is true that the icy corridors of water directly north of the town are the equivalent of a motorway for whale traffic with over a quarter of the world's species passing through. Most whale-watching boat owners, both here and in Reykjavík, are so confident that you will spot at least one of these massive creatures that you get a free trip if you don't.

However, you don't have to travel all the way to the north of Iceland to go whale-watching. There are good trips directly from Reykjavík harbour with an equally impressive success rate, and many operators in the smaller western and northern Iceland towns also.

Gentle Giants (*The Harbour, Húsavík. Tel: 464 1500. www.gentlegiants.is*) is a well-established company that operates daily, weather permitting.

Seatours (*Ólafsvík but book at the harbour at Stykkishólmur. Tel: 438 1450.*

www.seatours.is) sets out from the Snæfellsnes Peninsula.

Elding Whales & Puffin Island Tours (*Reykjavík old harbour. Tel: 555 3565. www.elding.is*) is one of a number of operators in the capital.

White-water or river rafting

The glaciers that feed Iceland's numerous rivers offer exciting opportunities for white-water rafting, whether you can tackle high-category rapids or are just a beginner dipping your toes into the sport for the first time. Boat guides are highly experienced, and companies can cater from easy through moderate to difficult, with the lower age limit ranging from 12 to 18 years.

Arctic Rafting (*Laugavegur 11, Reykjavík. Tel: 571 2200. www.arcticrafting.is*) offers trips of varying levels of difficulty.

Whale-watching trips from Reykjavík almost guarantee sightings

The Icelandic horse

The Icelandic horse has a special place in the hearts of all Icelanders. Brought by the first Norse settlers, they were invaluable for transport and farming and still serve as a useful mode of transport today, particularly for the yearly sheep round-up, or *réttir*, as they can go where no car can over the volcanic and mountainous terrain. Despite Icelandic farmers' reliance on mechanical machinery and the vast exodus of the population to Reykjavík, the horse is thriving and numbers over 100,000. As you travel around Iceland, watching horses in the field is a good indication of which direction the wind is coming from. Icelandic horses have developed a habit of standing rear to the wind with their tails between their legs to keep their most delicate areas warm.

During the Viking era, the horse was both revered and treated as chattel and a source of food. In the pagan period, a prized horse might be buried with his master or have an epic tale recited in his honour; roasted horsemeat was, however, considered a delicacy at pagan festivals, when stallions were also pitted against each other for entertainment.

The Icelandic horse is classed as a separate breed (*Equus scandinavicus*). Once found across all Scandinavia, as the name suggests, the Icelandic stock is the only one to remain pure, thanks to its isolation. It has never been crossbred, unlike its Norwegian,

Wild horses grazing in the highlands

Swedish and Danish cousins. When the settlers arrived on the island, they chose the most hardy horses to make the sea-crossing, keeping the quality of the base population high. In 1200, the Alþing passed a law forbidding equine import and export to protect the bloodline. This makes Icelandic livestock much sought after by today's collectors, and prices for fine specimens can run into hundreds of thousands of króna.

Equus scandinavicus is smaller than many breeds, being halfway between the size of a full-grown horse and a Shetland pony, with a thick pelt and an average height of 1.3m (4ft) at the shoulder. In looks it is gamine with a copious mane and tail and a slightly rotund body, to help protect it from winter winds and biting insects. Individuals come in a multitude of shades from light champagne beige to jet black.

The breed character is known to be sensible, dependable and sure-footed so it is perfect for beginners and well suited to Iceland's terrain. One of the breed's famous quirks is that it has five gaits, unlike all but one other horse species (the rest have just four). As well as a walk, trot, canter and gallop, the horse can perform a *tölt*, somewhere between a run and a walk, where the rider doesn't feel any bouncing movement because the movement is so fluid. In horse shows,

The Icelandic horse

this is demonstrated by the rider carrying a glass of wine at the same time – which isn't spilt at all.

Many horses are still wild-bred, living out in the hills of the highlands and roaming freely like sheep. They are rounded up each autumn and the year's foals are sold at market.

THE ICELANDIC NATIONAL HORSE SHOW

The biennial Icelandic National Horse Show or Landsmót is held in June–July. It is a unique and unforgettable event and the largest involving Icelandic horses in the world. The best horses in the country are on view competing in various classes, including a *tölt* competition, racing and breeding shows. The Landsmót attracts horse lovers and international buyers as well as the country's top breeders, all of whom come to watch the best riders in the country compete on the most beautiful horses. It alternates locations; the next show in 2012 will be held in Hella, southern Iceland, known as prime horse-breeding territory.

Birdwatching

Iceland is one of the world's richest birdwatching environments. Although only 70 species breed regularly here, over 300 have been spotted in total. However, it is not the number of species but the sheer numbers of individuals that are the draw. The island has an invaluable ecosystem for native, breeding and migratory birds.

Pick up a copy of the *Icelandic Bird Guide* by Jo Hilmarsson (Mal og Menning pub) plus a pair of binoculars.

Where

All the locations mentioned here are easily accessible by road or easy walk, so they are perfect for the fledgling ornithologist or one who doesn't want to have to trek too far and off the beaten path.

Snæfellsnes Peninsula The southern coast around Arnarstapi is replete with kittiwakes and Arctic terns. Guillemots and fulmars breed close by at Þúfubjarg. On the north coast the glaucous gull is more prevalent. At Álftafjörður (Swan Fjord), east of Stykkishólmur, around 500 breeding pairs can be enjoyed.

Reykjanes Peninsula Just offshore from Reykjanes lighthouse at Elday Island is Iceland's largest gannet colony. Further north at the Hafnaberg cliffs are various species of auk. The northern tip of the peninsula at Garðskagi sees many migratory species in the spring and autumn.

The Westfjords The Látrabjarg cliffs in the southwest corner are the largest bird-nesting cliffs in Iceland with huge populations of puffins on the flatlands and a razorbill colony at the base.

The north Lake Mývatn supports vast populations of ducks including Barrow's goldeneye and harlequin, plus grebes, waders and divers.

The east The marshy delta of the Jökulsá á Dal River offers the largest whimbrel population in Iceland, plus

See puffins on the Látrabjarg cliffs

vast flocks of greylag and pink-footed geese. Just north of Höfn there is another breeding ground for the whooper swan.

The south Head to Breiðhamerkursandur to watch the largest great skua colony on the island, while Dyrhólæy offers puffins, terns and guillemots.

The Westman Islands The world's largest puffin-breeding colony, plus the northernmost breeding ground of Manx shearwater and storm and Leach's petrel.

Watching seabirds around Arnarstapi

When

Spring Birds start to stake their claim as early as February but continue to arrive through to the end of May. Cliffs and shorelines are awash with courting pairs while the skies provide an arena for ritual displays. Several species use Iceland as a stopover as they continue north into the Arctic Circle. This is one of the best times to come bird-spotting.

Summer Once breeding is over, many species return to sea and by mid-August the numbers of seabird drop dramatically. If you want to see puffins, you need to visit from May to August.

Some species need to spruce up their plumage before winter arrives, so often lie low and are difficult to spot.

Autumn As the days get shorter, migratory birds tend to gather together in preparation for the flight. Thus geese can be seen roosting in vast numbers inland, while species such as dunlins or sandpipers crowd the coastal shallows. Arctic species also return south for a short pit stop.

Winter In winter, birds move to the coastal fringes to escape the harsh interior. Eiders and gulls are the most common species, but cormorants, skuas and auks can also be seen. The occasional ptarmigan might be viewed inland but snow buntings are more common.

Note: environmental protection

Iceland has many ground-breeding species. Take care to stay on the footpaths when out walking. Some areas are closed during the breeding season. Please abide by local by-laws as these protect delicate breeding grounds.

Food and drink

Iceland has gained a reputation in recent years for fine dining. A generation of young chefs and restaurateurs have taken modern fusion cuisine and made it their own. One consequence of the economic crisis has been a renewed focus on classic Icelandic cuisine made with locally sourced ingredients. Expect delicious lamb, salmon and seabirds.

Iceland's natural bounty can be distilled down to three foodstuffs – seafood, lamb and game. This triumvirate forms the basis of almost all the dishes on both traditional and modern menus.

Delicious smoked trout, pan-fried salmon, grilled lobster and fresh sushi make the most of the bounty of the sea. Whale meat can be found on some menus, or you can try *hákarl* (putrefied shark) – now considered a delicacy.

You cannot travel anywhere in Iceland without spotting hundreds of sheep. These graze freely on the wild grasses and herbs of the hills and mountains and this imparts a wonderful aromatic flavour to the meat, acting like a natural marinade. Simple grilled lamb is a standard on Icelandic menus but for specialist treats, try *svið* (blackened sheep's head) or *slátur* (parts of sheep minced and stuffed in a sheep's stomach).

Game comes in many forms, some of which may not suit bird lovers. Reindeer is the strongly flavoured

meat, while seabirds comprise the winged variety with guillemot and puffin being served in a variety of guises – don't forget that Iceland sees millions of these birds throughout the summer, so it is not surprising that they have become an important source of food.

Prices are on the high side by European standards. This is partly explained by the need to import the majority of foodstuffs. Petrol stations around the island offer a good budget eating option. There is always a café on-site serving snacks and grill-type meals – they offer good value even if the menu is a little repetitive.

The king of fast food in Iceland is the *pýlsur* – a sausage and bread ensemble much like a hot-dog, with a range of accompaniments from relish to cold, crunchy raw or fried onions. These offer much the best value for a quick lunch or afternoon snack, and you can buy them at kiosks around Reykjavík or at fuel stations.

Food and drink

Drinks

Coffee is king in Iceland and good coffee houses perform the same role as bars or pubs in other countries (*see p152*). *Skyr*, a drink made from skimmed milk flavoured with berries, is very refreshing in summer. Alcohol is very expensive, but not local beers like Egils Gull and Viking or the distilled vodka-like Brennivín that is made from potatoes. Brennivín is a good and common accompaniment to a taster of *hákarl* in restaurants.

Vegetarians

Reykjavík has a small selection of vegetarian restaurants (*see p172*) which should keep those on a short visit happy, but if you are travelling around the island choice is generally non-existent.

An abundance of fresh vegetables has only arrived in relatively recent years so the Icelandic diet has always focused on meat.

The fish eater won't have a problem as there's always a choice of seafood on any menu – including a lot of delicious sushi – but vegans will have to get creative.

MENU DECODER

Hákarl – putrefied shark meat
Hangikjöt – smoked lamb
Harðfiskur – dried haddock eaten as a snack, a little like beef jerky
Karfi – perch
Kartöfl – potatoes
Kjötsúpa – lamb stew
Lundi – puffin
Rauðkál – pickled cabbage
Silð – herring
Skarkoli – plaice
Skyr – a thick drink or dessert made from skimmed milk, and sometimes with yoghurt culture, flavoured with berries
Slátur – sheep's offal cooked in sheep's stomach
Soðning – boiled fish (served with potatoes)
Svið – blackened sheep's head cooked and served hot or cold

Enjoying a glacier-top buffet at the Langjökull ice cap

Food and drink

Prices indicate dinner for one without drinks:

★   under ISK 2,000
★★   ISK 2,000–4,000
★★★   ISK 4,000–6,000
★★★★ over ISK 6,000

Reykjavík

Á Næstu Grösum ★
Considered the best of the vegetarian bunch with a good-value set meal daily.
Laugavegur 20b.
Tel: 552 8410.
www.anaestugrosum.is

Bæjarins Beztu Pýlsur ★
City dwellers will tell you that this unassuming kiosk makes the best *pýlsur* in Reykjavík. You may need to queue but for the tastiest Icelandic hot-dog (made from lamb) it's worth it.
Tryggvagata 101.
Tel: 894 4515. www.bbp.is

Café Garðurinn ★
More of a relaxed coffee-shop-style atmosphere with a vegetarian menu.
Klapparstígur 37.
Tel: 561 2345.

Grænn Kostur ★
A vegetarian café with tasty snacks and meals to eat in or take away.
Skólavörðustígur 8.
Tel: 552 2028.

Hamborgarabulla Tomasar ★
Housed in a quirky monument building, this legendary hamburger restaurant has iconic status in the city. The chips are crisp, the burgers juicy. Try the espresso shake. There is another location in Egilsstaðir.
Geirsgata 1.
Tel: 511 1888.

Icelandic Fish & Chips ★
Enjoy the English tradition with an Icelandic spin: a choice of three or four different fish each day, dipped in a spelt batter, and served with a choice of sauces made with a *skyr* base.
Tryggvagata 8.
Tel: 511 1118.
www.fishandchips.is

Hornið ★★
A cosy restaurant near the harbour. Pizza is the house speciality, but the lasagne is also renowned among locals.
Hafnarstræti 115.
Tel: 551 3340.
www.hornid.is

Austur-Indíafjelagið ★★★
Fine Indian dining offering a selection of tandoori dishes and favourites like lamb vindaloo. The exotic spices are shipped directly from India.
Hverfisgata 56. Tel: 552 1630. www.austurindia.is

Islenskibarinn ★★★
This bar on Austurvöllur Square serves everything from bar snacks of dried fish to three-course set menus, taking inspiration from the sea and countryside. The bar came into being after the 'riots' following the economic crash; it's a way of celebrating all that's good about the country. As good for coffee and cakes as meals.
Pósthússtræti 9. Tel: 578 2020. www.icelandicbar.is

Silfur ★★★
Hotel Borg's restaurant is all Philippe Starck furniture and Michelin-star-styled food, served

up on slate plates. Lamb, salmon and local delicacies are best. *Pósthússtræti 11. Tel: 578 2008. www.silfur.is*

Humarhúsið (Lobster House) ★★★★
Housed in a wooden bungalow dating from the early 1900s, the speciality here is the delicate Icelandic langoustine. *Amtmannsstigur 1. Tel: 561 3303. www.humarhusid.is*

Sjávarkjallarinn ★★★★
The 'Seafood Cellar' is an award-winning restaurant serving Icelandic/Asian fusion cuisine in a cool neon-lit cellar dining room. *Aðalstræti 2. Tel: 511 1212. www.sjavarkjallarinn.is*

Outside Reykjavík
Greifinn ★
A good and popular reasonably budget option in the centre of Akureyri, offering fast food, a salad buffet and a range of full meals. *Glerárgötu 20, Akureyri. Tel: 460 1600. www.greifinn.is*

Gamli Baukur ★★
This timber chalet down on Húsavík's harbour is always busy around lunchtime with people from whale-watching trips – the terrace is a great place to watch the sea-traffic come and go. The menu has soups, salads and main courses, concentrating on seafood. *Hafn, Húsavík. Tel: 464 2442. www.gamlibaukur.is*

Narfeyrarstofa Sjávarloftið ★★★
The restaurant's name means 'ocean floor' and the menu concentrates on fruits of the sea. The dining room is a warm but modern wooden-clad loft area, while the ground floor is a café. *Aðalgötu 3, Stykkishólmur. Tel: 438 1119. www.narfeyrarstofa.is*

The Red Room Restaurant at Hotel Glymur ★★★
This unexpected restaurant is situated on a hill above Hvalfjörður, just 30km (19 miles) from Reykjavík. The kitchen specialises in

fresh Icelandic products prepared in innovative ways. Try the 'Taste of Glymur', a mixed plate of fish, meat and vegetables. Highland lamb, local beef and duck are also served. *Hotel Glymur, Hvalfjörður, Akranes. Tel: 430 3100. www.glymurresort.com*

Hotel Buðir ★★★★
One of Iceland's gourmet highlights, the service and food are excellent here – book in advance. Expect locally sourced lamb, fish and seafood and inventive desserts in a wonderful antique-styled dining room. *365 Snæfellsnes. Tel: 435 6700. www.budir.is*

Restaurant 4 at Hotel Rangá ★★★★
Overlooking the East Ranga salmon river, this modern Scandinavian-style restaurant is the best in the south of Iceland, serving up local delicacies such as fish soup and smoked puffin as well as delicious lamb and even kangaroo. *851 Hella. Tel: 487 5700. www.hotelranga.is*

Accommodation

Accommodation in Iceland is expensive and the hotel industry is still developing. Most of the upmarket hotels are to be found in the capital. There are a small number of comfortable properties scattered around the island, backed up by seasonal B&Bs and guesthouses. Tourist offices can provide information and accommodation guides. Budget travellers and hikers should consider the excellent YHA network.

For hotels it is important to make a booking from June to August, as space is limited. B&Bs are plentiful in Reykjavík but the standards vary. Prices are highest in summer and can drop by 40 per cent in winter.

SUGGESTED HOTELS

Peak-season prices per double room:
* ★ under ISK 15,000
* ★★ ISK 15,000–40,000
* ★★★ over ISK 40,000

Nationwide

Edda Hotels ★★★

These 13 summer hotels started out using students' rooms in boarding schools for visitor accommodation in summer. Many also have 'sleeping-bag space', for those who carry their own bedding. Recently, the group has branched out into custom-built hotel properties, often in more remote areas.
Tel: 444 4000.
http://hoteledda.is

Reykjavík

Apartment K ★

Live like a local in these excellent and well-priced flats scattered throughout Reykjavík. Design is a big theme and all apartments have their own cooking facilities, which can help to keep the cost down. Good for families and groups of friends.
Hverfisgata and various locations in the 101 district. Tel: 864 5719.
www.apartmentk.is

Reykjavík Youth Hostel ★

Part of the Hostelling International chain, there are two great hostels in Reykjavík, the eco-conscious one at Laugardalur and a smaller one in the city centre. Both offer single and double rooms as well as shared dorms, plus excursions, bus passes, bike and car hire. Join Hostelling International for the best rates. Other youth hostels in the HI chain across Iceland include turf-roofed houses and traditional corrugated-iron-clad cottages.
Sundlaugavegur 34, Laugardalur, and Vesturgata 17.
Tel: 553 8110.
www.hihostels.com

Hilton Reykjavík Nordica ★★

Contemporary hotel just outside the centre of Reykjavík towards Laugardalur Valley. All mod cons including VOX restaurant, a top-class health spa and breakfasts that draw non-residents. Good business facilities, too. *Suðurlandsbraut 2. Tel: 444 5000. www.hilton.com*

Radisson Blu Saga Hotel ★★

Well-appointed modern hotel with great facilities, popular with business travellers. Scandic design throughout, close to a thermal pool and within walking distance of the 101 district. The Grillið restaurant has long been one of the city's best. Great views from nearly all the rooms. *Hagatorg. Tel: 525 9900. www.radissonblu.com*

101 Hotel ★★★

Superior design hotel in a concrete building (it gets better inside) in central Reykjavík. The most stylish and luxurious place in town. Toiletries in the rooms are by Aveda and Blue Lagoon. The bar and restaurant are worth a visit in their own right. *Hverfisgata 10. Tel: 580 0101. www.101hotel.is*

Hotel Borg ★★★

Iconic Art Deco hotel on Austurvöllur Square with a long history dating back to a boxer. Catherine Deneuve is just one of many celebs to have stayed here; the Tower Suite is an incredibly romantic option, with views of the city and Mount Esja. Silfur restaurant is cutting edge. *Pósthússtræti 11. Tel: 551 1440. www.hotelborg.is*

Outside Reykjavík

Fire and Ice Guesthouse ★

Frost og Funi, or Fire and Ice, owns two different properties, one in Hveragerði and one near Höf, in Öræfi district. The Hveragerði property sits on the banks of a river and has 14 bright, modern rooms, pool and hotpot. The Öræfi guesthouse is close to Jökulsárlón and Skaftafell National Park. *Tel: 483 4959 (Hveragerði), 478 2260 (Öræfi). www.frostogfuni.is*

Hotel Eldhestar ★★

This country hotel at one of the oldest horse farms in Hveragerði pays homage to the Icelandic horse. There is also sleeping-bag accommodation available in cottages on the grounds. The restaurant serves tasty, simple cooking, with soup and sandwiches available at lunchtime. An ideal place to do some riding and explore the nearby thermal fields 30 minutes from Reykjavík; pick-ups can be arranged. *Vellir. Tel: 480 4800. www.hoteleldhestar.is*

Hotel Glymur ★★

This hotel's colourful proprietors have created an oasis of comfort high on a mountain above the scenic 'whale fjord'. Just a 45-minute drive from Reykjavík via route 47 and the Hvalfjörður

tunnel in the town of Akranes, where you can hike, ride a horse or bathe at the local swimming pool. The split-level rooms are well furnished and you can enjoy the night skies while sitting in a hot tub. Excellent restaurant on the premises.
Akranes. Tel: 430 3100.
www.glymurresort.com

Northern Light Inn ★★
This is an ideal spot if you want to pay a visit to the Blue Lagoon and have an early flight the next morning – just 15 minutes from the airport and a short stroll to the lagoon. From September to April you may experience the magic of the Northern Lights. The 32 rooms have cosy down quilts. Sumptuous buffet breakfast is served in Kristjana's Kitchen, the on-site restaurant run by the proprietress. Complimentary Blue Lagoon and airport shuttles also available.
Grindavíkurbraut 1, Grindavík.
Tel: 426 8650.
www.northernlightinn.is

Snæfellsnes and the Westfjords
Hotel Breiðafjorður ★
This small hotel in the centre of Stykkishólmur is minutes from the harbour, restaurants and post office. The 11 rooms are basic and comfortable and the staff are friendly.
Aðalgata 8, Stykkishólmur.
Tel: 433 2200.
http://hotelbreidafjordur.is

Hotel Búðir ★★★
This luxury inn (*see p80*) is surrounded by lava fields, a black-sand beach, a 19th-century church and views of the Snæfellsjökull glacier. The rooms are individually decorated with antiques and cosy details. The restaurant has a serene, candlelit atmosphere for intimate dining and some of the best food in the country. An unforgettable experience.
365 Snæfellsnes.
Tel: 430 3100.
www.budir.is

Northern Iceland
Gistiheimilið Árból ★★
The lovely 100-year-old timber mansion which is

now a guesthouse has great character with pretty rooms, and a garden with a river at the end.
Ásgarðsvegi 2, Húsavík.
Tel: 464 2220.
http://arbol.1.is

Hotel Harpa ★★
This modern, quiet and comfortable hotel (linked to the Hotel Kea) in the city centre has 26 well-equipped rooms and serves a good breakfast.
Hafnarstræti 87–89, Akureyri.
Tel: 460 2000.
www.keahotels.is

Hotel Reynihlið ★★
This family-run hotel at Lake Mývatn has 41 rooms. More like an old-fashioned boarding house than a hotel, the rooms are comfortable and the Myllan (Mill) restaurant serves up a selection of lamb, fish or veggie dishes. There is also an adjacent tavern, Gamlibær, that serves up more simple fare: soup, sandwiches and cakes.

660 Mývatn.
Tel: 464 4170.
www.reynihlid.is

Eastern Iceland

Gistihúsið
Egilsstöðum ★★

This romantic guesthouse is in Egilsstaðir, located at the most frequented crossroads in eastern Iceland. Family-run, it dates to 1903 and the 18 charming rooms have the usual amenities. Located in a beauty spot along the lake and next to a horse farm, there is also a fine restaurant on the premises.
Egilsstaðir. Tel: 471 1114.
www.egilsstadir.com

Hotel Aldan ★★

Located in a beauty spot overlooking a calm fjord rich in birdlife near Seyðisfjörður, Hotel Aldan used to be the town's bank and has been furnished with antiques and handcrafted textiles to create the timeless ambience of the past. The intimate restaurant is housed in one of Iceland's oldest stores and serves fresh fish

caught daily with vegetables from a local ecological farm. The neighbouring Hotel Snæfell – a three-storey wooden house built in 1908 by the mouth of the river – is under the same ownership.
Norðurgata 2, Seyðisfjörður.
Tel: 472 1277.
www.hotelaldan.com

Southern Iceland

Hotel Anna ★

This small family-run farmhouse between Seljalandsfoss and Skógafoss is located in a former cowshed and stables, lovingly restored with antiques. Each room is en-suite with TV and phone. The breakfast buffet includes home-baked treats, and dinner is also available.
Moldnúpi. Tel: 487 8950.
www.hotelanna.is

Hotel Hvolsvöllur ★★

This hotel in the heart of Saga country has 50 en-suite rooms in a new wing and 4 rooms in the original building. They have a good restaurant and are in close

proximity to a swimming pool, golf course, stable and fishing lake.
Hliðarvegi 7.
Tel: 487 8050.
www.hotelhvolsvollur.is

Hotel Þórshamar ★★

Simple hotel accommodation in the centre of town in Heimæy on the Westman Islands. Best of a basic bunch, this hotel has a whirlpool, sauna, lounge and pool room. Book ahead in summer.
Vestmannabraut 28, Heimæy. Tel: 481 2900.
http://
hotelvestmannaeyjar.is

Hotel Rangá ★★★

Dubbed one of the world's best Northern-Lights-watching spots (you can even do it from their hotpots). This luxury country hotel has its own stuffed polar bear, simple country rooms and exquisite, slightly mad suites taking inspiration from the seven continents. Volcano viewing and helicopter tours recommended.
851 Hella. Tel: 487 5700.
www.hotelranga.is

Practical guide

Arriving

Entry formalities

Citizens of the following countries can enter Iceland without a visa provided their passport is valid for three months after the end of their stay: EU countries, Australia, Canada, New Zealand, Switzerland, Great Britain (including Bermuda, Turks and Caicos Islands, Cayman Islands, Anguilla, Montserrat, British Virgin Islands, St Helena, Falkland Islands and Gibraltar), the USA. Iceland is part of the Schengen agreement so although it isn't an EU member, similar entry procedures apply, i.e. most European visitors can stay for up to 90 days without a visa.

Visas

Countries not covered by the Schengen agreement will need a visa. These are available from local Danish embassies. Consult Iceland's immigration website for further advice (*www.utl.is*).

Arriving by air

The main airport of entry is Keflavík International (*Tel: 426 6000. www.kefairport.is*), 40km (25 miles) southwest of Reykjavík. In addition, since 2010 European flights have also flown to Akureyri airport in northern Iceland in summer (*Tel: 424 4000. http://flugstodir.is*).

Icelandair (*www.icelandair.com*) is the national carrier offering a network of services to major cities throughout western Europe and northern USA. There are no direct flights from Australia or New Zealand to Iceland. Multiple-ticket combinations for flights into Europe and onward to Reykjavík are possible.

Iceland Express (*www.icelandexpress. com*) has budget flights from the UK and Europe to Reykjavík departing all year round and to Akureyri in the summer. They also fly to New York via Reykjavík.

Flybus links the international airport at Keflavík with Reykjavík. The buses are timed to meet all incoming flights. Passengers are taken to the BSÍ Bus Terminal where they board a shuttle bus to their hotel. Tickets cost around ISK 3,500.

The Leifur Eiríksson Air Terminal at Keflavík International Airport has extensive facilities. The departure area offers shops, restaurants, recreation options and general airport services. The duty-free selection has a diverse offering, from Icelandic and Scandinavian design items to warm weather clothing and electronic equipment. Note that you can buy duty-free items on entry as well as exit from the country. The Flybus to Reykjavík is directly outside (*see above*), and tickets can be bought on the right side of the terminal by the exit. The Landsbanki service desk for currency exchange is near the exit at the right of the terminal. There is also a small tourist information office on arrival.

Practical guide

Arriving by sea

Smyril Line runs a weekly 1,500-vehicle ferry all the year round linking Seyðisfjörður on the east coast of Iceland, the Faroe Islands, Sweden and Denmark. Contact Smyril Line, Faroe Islands (*PO Box 370, FR 110 Tórshavn. Tel: 298 345 900. www.smyril-line.fo*) for details (*see also p188*).

Camping

Camping is popular, and there are sites in most towns and in national parks and areas of natural beauty. Some farms also offer camping space. Facilities at most sites are basic with a small toilet/shower block and a couple of sinks. Power is not normally provided. Sites may become overcrowded in high season (June–August), and most close mid-September to the end of May. Most sites are close to small supermarkets where you can buy provisions. There are 29 motorhome waste-dump sites around the island, situated at campsites and some petrol stations.

For more details, contact the Iceland Environment and Food Agency (*Suðurlandsbraut 24, 108 Reykjavík. Tel: 591 2000. www.ust.is*). The website *www.nat.is* also has a list of campsites across the country.

Children

Make sure that children are adequately protected against the weather. In cold weather, have hat and gloves ready, plus a waterproof and warm outer layer. In sunny weather, protect their skin with high-factor sunblock even if the temperature doesn't seem warm.

Climate

Despite its northerly position, the coastline of Iceland has a remarkably mild climate. It benefits from the Gulf Stream, which keeps the air relatively benign – cool in summer and mild in winter, although you can find sharp winds, rain and snow in any season.

In summer, the average temperature is 11°C (52°F) with occasional warmer spells. In winter, temperatures average at around freezing point (comparable to New York). At all times of the year

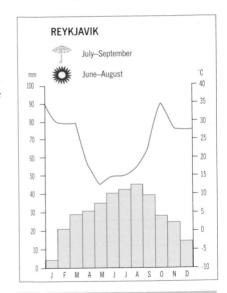

REYKJAVIK
July–September
June–August

WEATHER CONVERSION CHART
25.4mm = 1 inch
°F = 1.8 × °C + 32

the weather can change frequently. (*Weather information in English: Tel: 902 0600. www.vedur.is*)

Crime

When you visit Iceland you are at relatively low risk of being a victim of serious crime. However, so-called petty crime such as theft can be a problem in Reykjavík, especially from vehicles. Crime is almost non-existent in the small towns in the rest of the island. Precautions to minimise your chances of a loss include:

• Do not leave valuables in a car and leave nothing on display.
• Don't carry large amounts of cash or valuables with you.
• Deposit valuables in the hotel safe.
• Take extra care at cashpoint machines – don't allow bystanders to see your PIN.
• Don't leave valuables unattended in cafés and restaurants.

Customs regulations

Duty-free rules are set out below. Over-20s are allowed to take in the following items duty free:

• 1 litre (1¾pt) of wine or 6 litres (10½pts) of beer.
• 1 litre (1¾pt) of stronger alcohol.
• If no spirits and beer, then 2.5 litres (4⅓pts) of wine can be imported.
• Over-18s can also take 200 cigarettes or 250g (9oz) of tobacco.

There are no currency restrictions. Angling and riding gear must be disinfected and certified as such by a qualified veterinarian before it can be used in the country, otherwise it will be disinfected at the owner's expense.

Driving

Driving around in Iceland can be a challenge but is generally not difficult provided you exercise care and caution. Roads are a mixture of asphalt and compacted dirt surfaces and you may pass from one to the other regularly – the transition area between the two (signposted *Malbik endar*) requires extra care. The minimum age for driving a hire car is 21 years, and 25 years for a jeep.

Iceland drives on the right, overtaking on the left. Speed limits are 50kph (31mph) in urban areas, 80kph (50mph) on gravel roads and 90kph (56mph) on asphalt surfaces, but in some local streets speeds may drop to 30kph (19mph). Speed bumps are common at town limits. It is forbidden to drive off prescribed roads and lanes.

Seat belts are compulsory for all passengers including passengers on tour buses. Headlights must be on at all times when the vehicle is in motion (day or night). Motorists are not allowed to drive after drinking alcohol and the law is strictly enforced.

Most bridges on the island are single-lane (signposted *Einbreið brú*) and when oncoming traffic approaches it is the first car there that has priority. If in any doubt, let oncoming traffic have priority.

On dirt roads, traffic normally rides in the middle of the road until other traffic approaches, so flying stones can be a problem when overtaking or passing oncoming traffic.

There are many blind rises on roads (signposted *Blindhæð*). Make sure you keep to the right when approaching these crests.

Look out for fast-moving 4WD trucks or slow-moving farm vehicles. Sheep wander freely, so slow down as you approach them. Also, slow down for people on horseback.

A special mention must be made about the highland roads of the interior. These must not be attempted in a 2WD vehicle as the surfaces and ground clearances are not suitable. These areas also have limited mobile-phone reception – don't risk getting lost or breaking down.

Weather is a major factor when driving in Iceland. Rain and ice can make road surfaces slippery and low cloud can shorten visibility, especially on mountain passes. Roads can be closed because of weather conditions at all times of year and closed throughout the winter (October–May), so ask about the conditions before travelling.

For information on current conditions of all Iceland's roads, tel: 522 1000. www.vegagerdin.is

Fuel

Most major towns have a choice of petrol stations while smaller settlements have one source – this usually comes with a general store and

CONVERSION TABLE

FROM	TO	MULTIPLY BY
Inches	Centimetres	2.54
Feet	Metres	0.3048
Yards	Metres	0.9144
Miles	Kilometres	1.6090
Acres	Hectares	0.4047
Gallons	Litres	4.5460
Ounces	Grams	28.35
Pounds	Grams	453.6
Pounds	Kilograms	0.4536
Tons	Tonnes	1.0160

To convert back, for example from centimetres to inches, divide by the number in the third column.

MEN'S SUITS

UK	36	38	40	42	44	46	48
Rest of Europe	46	48	50	52	54	56	58
USA	36	38	40	42	44	46	48

DRESS SIZES

UK	8	10	12	14	16	18
France	36	38	40	42	44	46
Italy	38	40	42	44	46	48
Rest of Europe	34	36	38	40	42	44
USA	6	8	10	12	14	16

MEN'S SHIRTS

UK	14	14.5	15	15.5	16	16.5	17
Rest of Europe	36	37	38	39/40	41	42	43
USA	14	14.5	15	15.5	16	16.5	17

MEN'S SHOES

UK	7	7.5	8.5	9.5	10.5	11
Rest of Europe	41	42	43	44	45	46
USA	8	8.5	9.5	10.5	11.5	12

WOMEN'S SHOES

UK	4.5	5	5.5	6	6.5	7
Rest of Europe	38	38	39	39	40	41
USA	6	6.5	7	7.5	8	8.5

A prettily situated tourist information office

café. Note that a small number of fuel stations do not have a shop/café. Fuel can be purchased after hours via the credit card machine at the pump. Keep your vehicle well fuelled as distances between pumps can be long.

Car hire

Cars can be hired at Keflavík airport, in Reykjavík or at domestic airports. A 4WD vehicle is strongly advised if you intend to travel into the highlands to cope with the rough conditions; 2WD compact cars are suitable for routes following the ring road. Note that if you hire a 2WD vehicle and attempt routes only suitable for 4WD vehicles, your car insurance will become void. If you rent a 4WD vehicle, your insurance will not be valid for fording water.

There are local and international agencies but the company with the largest network is Hertz. They have offices at most major centres and offer the best backup if you have a problem.

Your domestic driving licence is recognised in Iceland. You will need to have had a full licence for at least one year and be over 21 to hire a vehicle; most hire companies require you to be 23 to hire a 4WD vehicle.

You will need a credit card to stand for a deposit.

Bringing your own vehicle into Iceland

Carry the registration document, valid insurance and valid licence. A temporary import permit valid for one month will be issued at your port of entry. This can be extended.

Electricity

Iceland uses 240V 50Hz for its supply. Plugs are the two-pinned variety, so travellers from the UK will need an adaptor.

Embassies

Embassies located in Reykjavík:
UK Embassy *Laufásvegur 31, 101 Reykjavík. Postal address: PO Box 460, 121 Reykjavík. Tel: 550 5100. http://ukiniceland.fco.gov.uk*
Vice Consul – Akureyri *Central Hospital (Fjordungssjukrahusid a Akureyri), v/Eyrarlandsveg. Postal address: PO Box 380, I S 602 Akureyri. Tel: 463 0102.*

US Embassy *Laufásvegur 21, 101 Reykjavík. Tel: 562 9100.* http://iceland.usembassy.gov
Australian Embassy
No embassy or consular representation
Canadian Embassy *Túngata 14. Postal address: PO Box 1510, 121 Reykjavík. Tel: 575 6500.* www.canadainternational.gc.ca
Republic of Ireland Honorary Consulate *Mr David Thorsteinsson, Ásbuð 106, Garðabaer. Tel: 554 2355.*
New Zealand
No embassy or consular representation
South Africa Honorary Consul *Borgatún 35. Postal address: PO Box 462, 105 Reykjavík. Tel: 591 0355.*

Emergency telephone numbers
For Ambulance, Fire and Police, available 24 hours a day, telephone *112*.

Health
There are no compulsory inoculations for travel to Iceland. Medical provision is of a high standard, with all staff speaking some English if not good English, but charges are expensive if you have not obtained an EHIC card (*see below*). Small settlements will have a local clinic and large towns a hospital.

UK and EU citizens must produce a European Health Insurance Card, available online at *www.ehic.org.uk*, by phoning *0845 605 0707* or from post offices, in order to obtain free treatment; otherwise, they will be charged and will need to reclaim the money on their return.

Citizens of other countries must pay at the time of treatment in local currency (take receipts to claim money back from your insurance company) unless they have insurance with a company that pays direct.

Pharmacies (*apótek*) sell many drugs over the counter; however, brand names vary, so if you need a specific medication/drug take an empty packet with you to aid the pharmacist or carry a prescription from your doctor.

Insurance
Having adequate insurance cover is vital (*see Health above*). UK citizens with a European Health Insurance Card will be treated without charge but a travel insurance policy will allow repatriation if the injury/illness warrants it. All other nationalities should ensure adequate cover for illness, as they will be charged at the point of treatment.

Insurance companies also usually provide cover for cancellation or travel delay. Check your policy carefully for exclusions related to volcanic or earthquake activity and quiz your insurance company closely. There is no uniform level of cover on this; volcanoes have recently led to delayed flights.

Language
The national language of Iceland is Icelandic, a Scandinavian language with Germanic roots (*see p185*). But don't worry – almost all Icelanders speak good English.

An Icelandic newspaper

Lost property

Icelanders are generally very honest people and will hand lost items in at cafés etc, so retrace your steps if you can, to see if your item can be found. If not, try the local police station. You will need an official police report to make an insurance claim for any lost property. If you lose your passport, contact your embassy or consulate immediately.

Maps

Most tourist offices produce good maps of their towns and regions for car tours. If you intend to do any hiking, a specialist map is advised. Landmælinger Íslands produce accurate maps for the whole of the island and they are available in tourist offices and bookshops.

Media

Iceland has three TV channels. Many programmes are broadcast in their native language with Icelandic subtitles, so there are lots of UK and American favourites. Large hotels have satellite TV, usually with CNN, BBC News 24 or Sky News channels.

There are no English-language mainstream newspapers printed in Iceland. International papers are available in newsagents/bookshops at Reykjavík and Akureyri.

Internet cafés and Wi-Fi hotspots are common.

The *Iceland Review* is an excellent quarterly magazine which can be bought in bookshops.

Money matters
Money

The Icelandic currency is the Icelandic króna, usually indicated by the initials ISK. Coins come in denominations of 100 kr, 50 kr, 10 kr, 5 kr and 1 kr, and banknotes in denominations of 5,000 kr, 2,000 kr, 1,000 kr and 500 kr.

All Icelandic banks provide foreign exchange. They are found in all major towns and are generally *open on weekdays from 9.15am to 4pm.* Many have extended hours on Friday and some are open on weekends. Travellers will find it easier if they carry US dollars, euros or pounds sterling, which are easier to change than other currencies. Hotels may provide an exchange service but their commission rates are expensive.

Traveller's cheques: Not as easy to cash as foreign currency, they can only be changed at banks (though they are more secure than cash as you can get them replaced if they get lost or stolen).

ATMs: ATMs are becoming more numerous and you will certainly be

Language

Pronunciation

All letters are pronounced as in English unless indicated below.

Capital	Small case	Pronunciation
Ð	ð	'th' as in feather
Þ	þ	'th' as in thing
Ý or Í	ý or í	'ee'
Á	á	'ow'
É	é	'ye' as in yes
Ó	ó	'o' as in wrote
Ö	ö	'e' as in stern
Æ	æ	'eye'
AU	au	'ur' of furry without the r
Ú	ú	the 'oo' of true
J	j	as 'y' in yes
DJ	dj	hard 'j' sound
F	f	as in English, but also 'v' in vain. Pronounced as an abrupt 'b' before an l or an n
HV	hv	'kv'
LL	ll	as in the 'ddl' in riddle
P	p	as in English but pronounced 'f' if before an s or a t
R	r	always rolled on the tongue

HELPFUL PHRASES

English	Icelandic
Hello	Hállo
Goodbye	Bless
Yes	Jái
No	Nei
Do you speak English?	Talar Þu ensku?
I don't understand	Ég skil ekki
Where is the...?	Hvar er...?
How much is it?	Hvar koster þetta?
Thank you	Takk fyrir
Do you have any vacancies?	Eru herbergi laus?
My name is	Ég heiti
Doctor	lækni
Dentist	tannlæknir

Tourist office	Upplýsingaþjónustu fyrir ferðafólk
Help!	Hjálp!
One	Einn
Two	Tveir
Three	Þrír
Four	Fjórir
Five	Fimm
Six	Sex
Seven	Sjö
Eight	Átta
Nine	Níu
Ten	Tíu
One hundred	Eitt hundrað

able to get cash in all the major Icelandic towns.

Credit cards

Credit cards are widely accepted across Iceland, and locals use plastic for even the smallest purchases. The most popular ones are MasterCard and Visa. You can use your credit card to get cash advances over the counter in banks.

Opening hours

Shops are open Monday–Thursday 10am–6pm, Friday till 7pm, Saturday 10am–4pm with extended hours in summer and in shopping malls in Reykjavík. Most shops are closed on Sundays. Some souvenir shops in Reykjavík and the shopping malls are open on Sundays 10am–6pm. Supermarkets are open 9am–9pm and some until 11pm. Banks remain open Monday–Friday 9.15am–4pm.

Museums have varying opening hours because many are private. Museums in the capital are generally open Monday–Saturday 10am–5pm (11am in winter), Sunday noon–5pm. Other museums are open June– September but check hours within this guide.

Pharmacies: As for shops. There are duty pharmacies in the major towns.

Police (Lögreglan)

Police wear navy-blue uniforms and routinely carry guns, though you rarely see them except in their cars. They are generally approachable for queries such as asking directions and most speak good English. The emergency telephone number is *112*.

Exploring Iceland in a 4WD

Post offices

Postal services are operated by the state-run HP, recognised by their red signs and postboxes. Main post offices are open Monday–Friday 8.30am–4.30pm. Smaller offices around the island may open slightly longer or shorter hours. In addition to this, in Reykjavík the post office at Grensásvegur 9 is open on Saturday 10am–2pm, and the post office at Þönglabakki 4 is open Monday–Friday 10am–6pm.

Public holidays

The following dates are official holidays in Iceland – most dates are movable, so check with the tourist office before you travel. All government buildings and banks and most commercial businesses will be closed on these days.

1 January New Year's Day
March/April Maundy Thursday (before Easter)
March/April Good Friday
March/April Easter Sunday
March/April Easter Monday
April/early May First day of summer
1 May May Day
Mid–late May Ascension Day
Mid-May–early June Whit Sunday
Mid-May–early June Whit Monday
17 June National Day
First Monday in August Bank Holiday Monday
24 December Christmas Eve (from midday)

25 December Christmas Day
26 December Boxing Day
31 December New Year's Eve (from midday)

Public transport

Air

Local air services run by Air Iceland and Eagle Air operate from Reykjavík to settlements around the island (as well as Greenland) with airfields at Akureyri, Egilsstaðir, Grímsey, Hornafjörður, Ísafjörður, Þórshöfn and Vopnafjörður. There are also combination air and bus vouchers with one way by air and return by bus. Routes are from the hub at Reykjavík.

Bus

In Reykjavík buses run Monday–Saturday 7am–midnight and Sunday 10am–midnight.

Bus services offer an efficient method of touring around and even run trips into the highlands during the summer, though distances and times can be long. The BSÍ Bus Terminal (*Vatnsmýrarvegi 10. Tel: 562 1011. www.bsi.is*) is the best source of information for vouchers, passes and routes touring Iceland, or ask at the Tourist Office.

Ferry

A well-managed fleet of ferries links the mainland with the outlying islands the year round. Details can be obtained from the harbour offices.

Bus and ferry timetables

The Thomas Cook European Rail Timetable is published monthly and gives the times of buses and ferries in Iceland. It is available to buy online at *www.thomascookpublishing.com*, from branches of Thomas Cook in the UK or by phoning *01733 416477*.

Sustainable tourism

Thomas Cook is a strong advocate of ethical and fairly traded tourism and believes that the travel experience should be as good for the places visited as it is for the people that visit. That's why we're a firm supporter of The Travel Foundation: a charity that develops solutions to help improve and protect holiday destinations, their environment, traditions and culture. To find out what you can do to make a positive difference to the places you travel to and the people who live there, please visit: *www.thetravelfoundation.org.uk*

Telephones

Modern hotels usually have a direct-dial phone system, but beware as they often charge huge surcharges to make calls. Ask about charges before you decide to ring home.

The country code for Iceland is *354*. All numbers have seven digits and there is no need to dial the country code once you are on the island.

Here are the main country codes, should you want to make an international call from Iceland:

USA and Canada *00 1*
UK *00 44*
Ireland *00 353*
Australia *00 61*
New Zealand *00 64*

There are three GSM operators in Iceland: Iceland Telecom, Islandssimi and TAL. They all sell prepaid phonecards and offer GSM services. GSM phones can be rented from Iceland Telecom (*Armúli 27, Reykjavík*).

Time

Iceland operates Greenwich Mean Time throughout the year, so in winter, if it is midday in Reykjavík, it is the same time in London, 7am in New York and Toronto. In summer, it is 1pm in London, 8am in New York or Toronto.

Tipping

Tipping is not expected in Iceland. Service and VAT are included, though a tip for service is not amiss.

Toilets

Toilets are generally clean and of a good standard. There are public facilities at

Sign showing speed limits

Take a boat ride on Jökulsárlón

all fuel stations and information centres. National parks and rural car parks also have toilets. In urban areas, visit a café/bar.

Tourist information

Every town has a well-equipped and helpful tourist information office that will help with information about excursions and accommodation. The Reykjavík offices also give a lot of information about other parts of the island.

The website *www.visiticeland.com* is an excellent source of information.

Travellers with disabilities

Provision for travellers with mobility problems is variable. New buildings have to meet a code of standard practice for wheelchair access. Always make specific enquiries at hotels if you require specially equipped rooms. Because of the very nature of its natural attractions, some areas of beauty will be difficult to access.

For more holiday and travel information for people with disabilities, contact Tourism for All (*Tel: 0845 124 9971 (UK)*. *www.tourismforall.org.uk*).

Practical guide

Index

Acknowledgements

The author and photographer would like to send thanks to Hjörvar S Högnason of Icelandair UK and Dóra Magnusdóttir at Visit Reykjavík for their invaluable help and enthusiasm during the research for this book.

For the 2010 update of this guide, Laura Dixon would like to thank Clair Horwood of the London branch of the Icelandic Tourist Board and Matt Hall for his driving, support and photography.

Thomas Cook Publishing wishes to thank PETE BENNETT, BIG WORLD PRODUCTIONS, to whom the copyright belongs, for the photographs in this book, except for the following images:
ÁRNI TORFASON 11, 33, 35, 36, 37, 39, 45, 47, 55, 60, 134, 149, 153, 154, 157
BLUE LAGOON 58, 146
FLICKR 27, 124 (Skender); 50 (Jennifer Boyer); 66 (big-ashb); 102, 150 (Ville Miettinen); 140, 162 (Jennifer Smith); 145 (ihn_picture)
ICELAND TOURIST BOARD 1, 25, 34, 43
MUSEUM OF ICELANDIC WITCHCRAFT AND SORCERY 81
MÝVATN NATURE BATHS 147
ROBERT HARDING WORLD IMAGERY 171 (Ragnar Sigurdsson/Robert Harding)
STOCK XCHNG 142 (Wim Delen)
THOMAS COOK PUBLISHING 42, 186
VISIT REYKJAVÍK 48, 54, 159
WIKIMEDIA 61, 141 (Andreas Tille); 63 (Chmeez); 68 (Tommy Bee); 70 (public domain); 75 (Carlos Ferrer); 103 (Jutta234); 121 (Thalion77); 131 (Chris 73); 168 (Aconcagua)
WORLD PICTURES/PHOTOSHOT 16

For CAMBRIDGE PUBLISHING MANAGEMENT LTD:
Project editor: Rosalind Munro
Typesetter: Trevor Double
Proofreaders: Kelly Walker & Karolin Thomas
Indexer: Amanda Jones

SEND YOUR THOUGHTS TO
BOOKS@THOMASCOOK.COM

We're committed to providing the very best up-to-date information in our travel guides and constantly strive to make them as useful as they can be. You can help us to improve future editions by letting us have your feedback. If you've made a wonderful discovery on your travels that we don't already feature, if you'd like to inform us about recent changes to anything that we do include, or if you simply want to let us know your thoughts about this guidebook and how we can make it even better – we'd love to hear from you.

Send us ideas, discoveries and recommendations today and then look out for your valuable input in the next edition of this title.

Emails to the above address, or letters to the traveller guides Series Editor, Thomas Cook Publishing, PO Box 227, Coningsby Road, Peterborough PE3 8SB, UK.

Please don't forget to let us know which title your feedback refers to!